Kawaii Sea Life Coloring Book

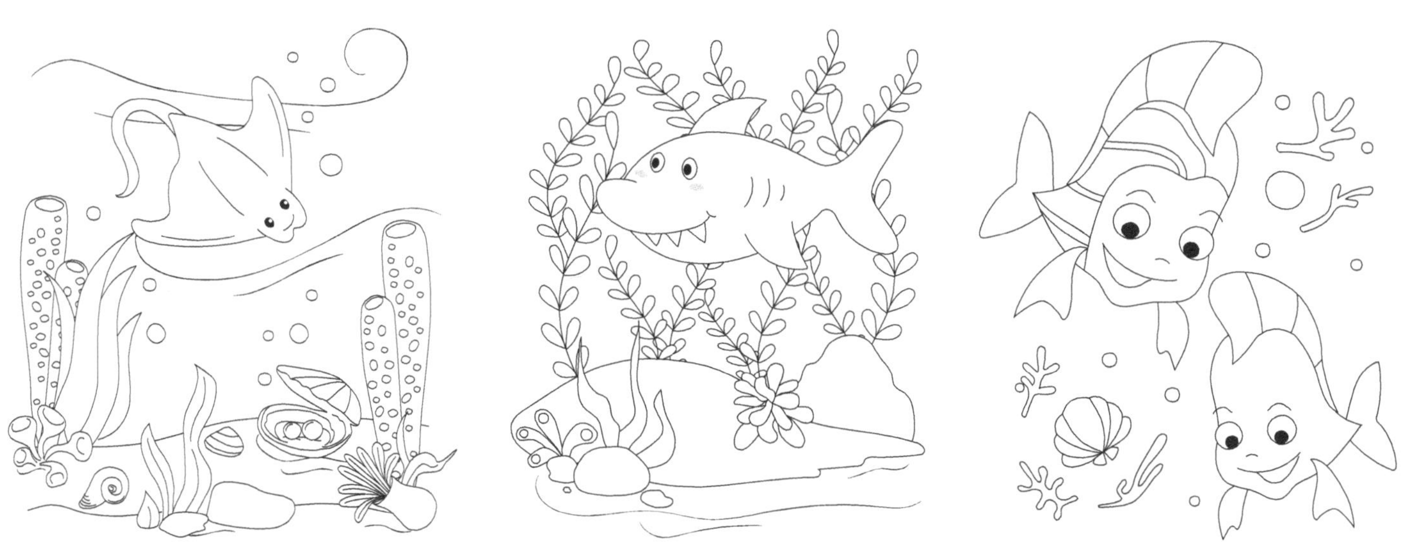

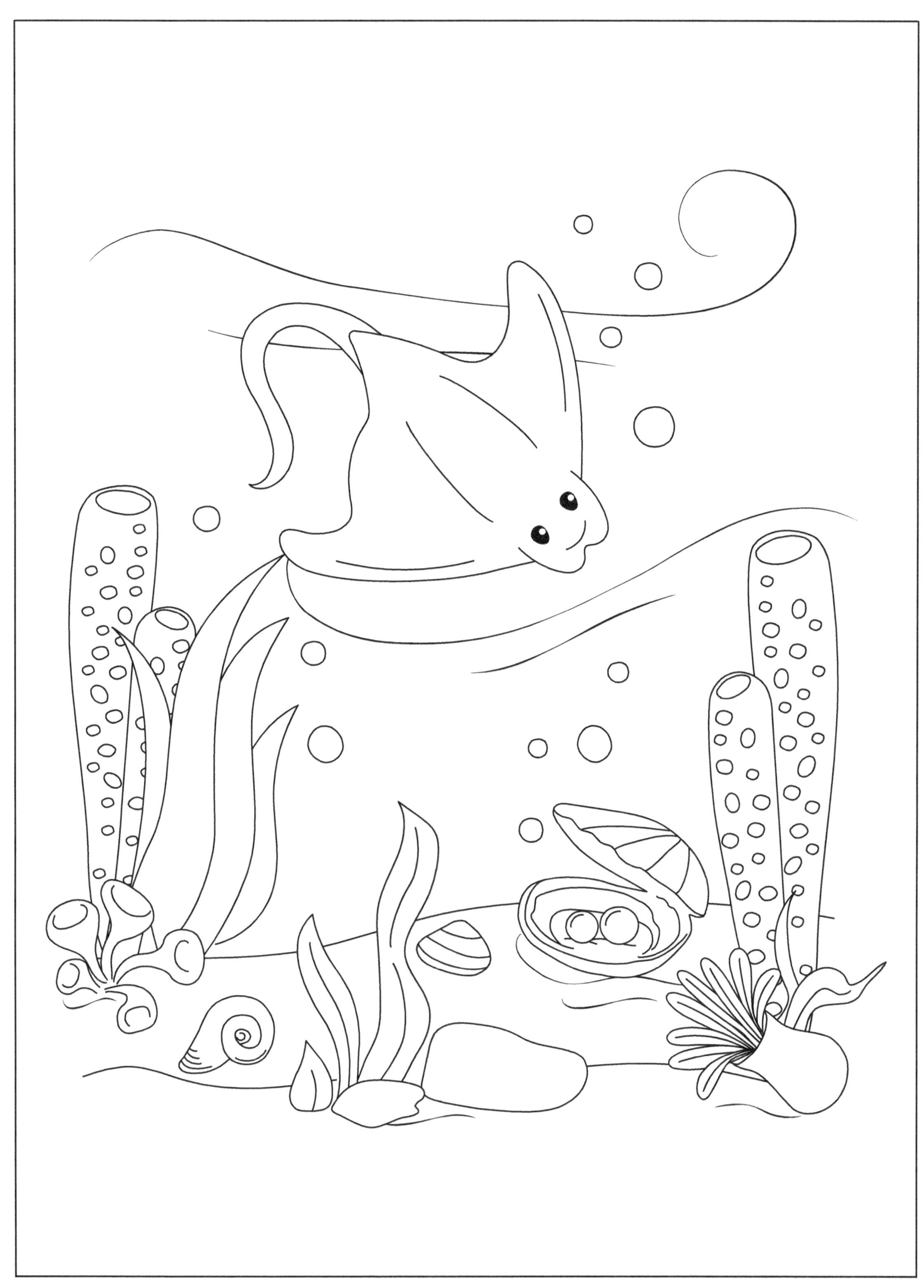

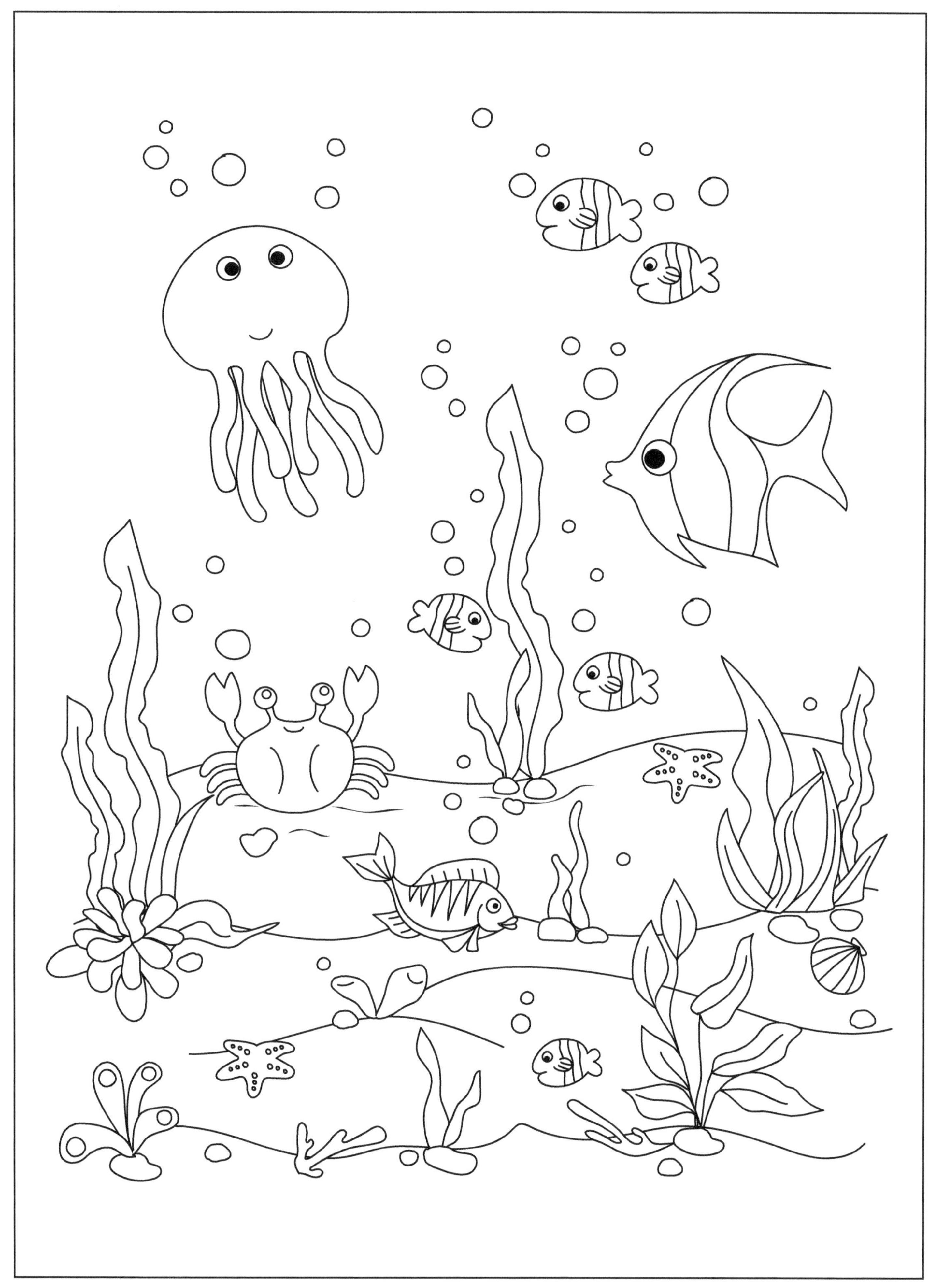

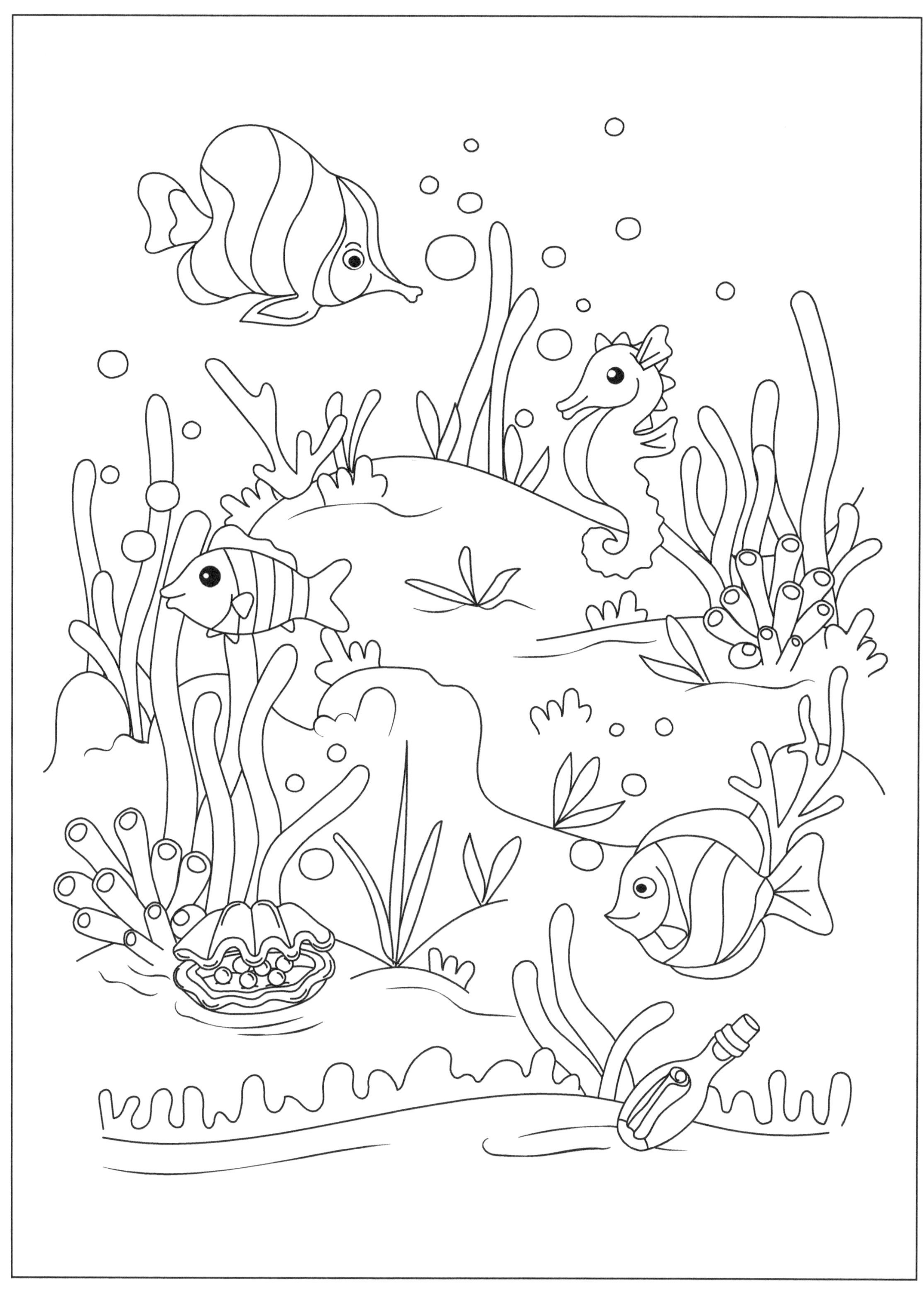

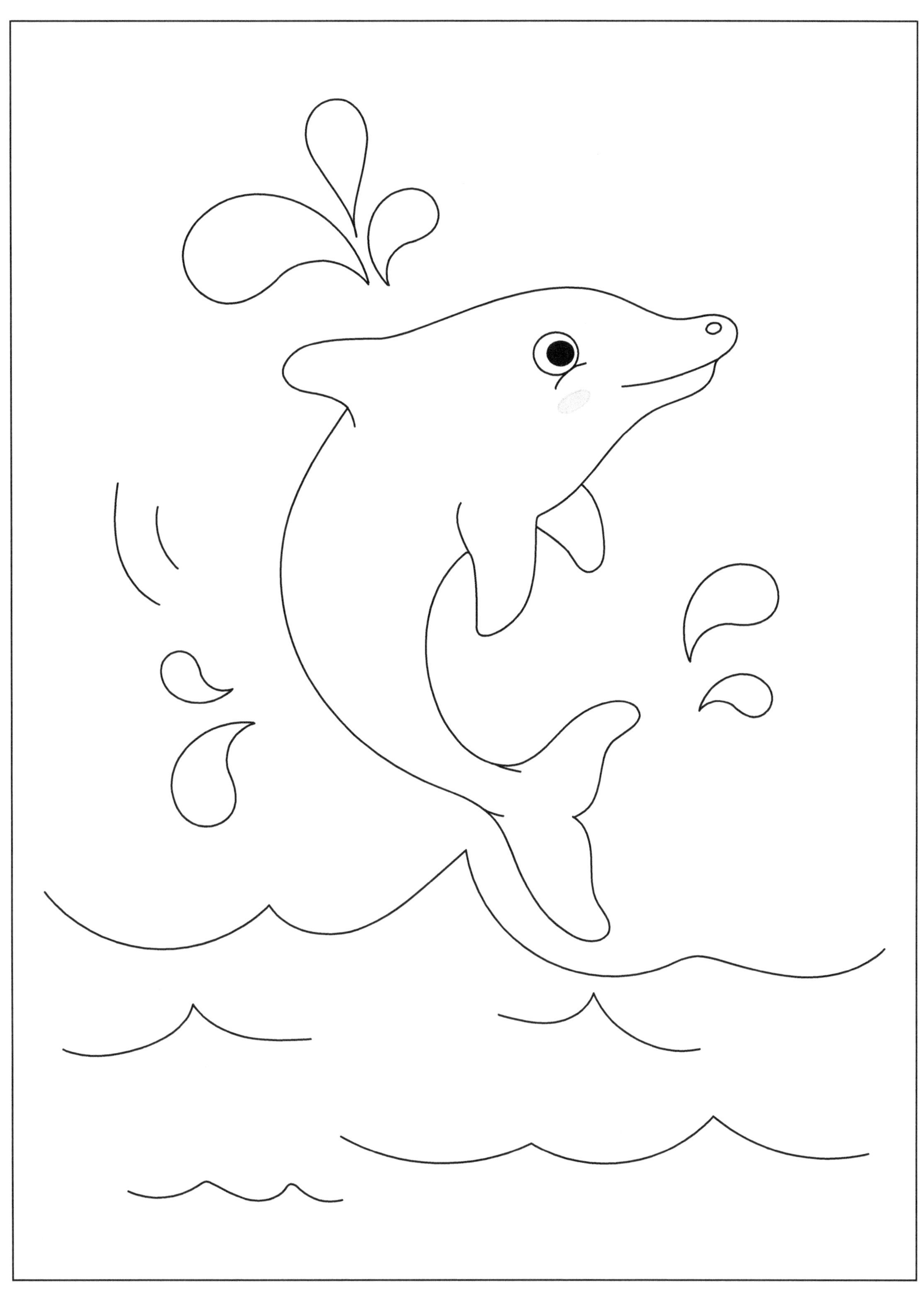

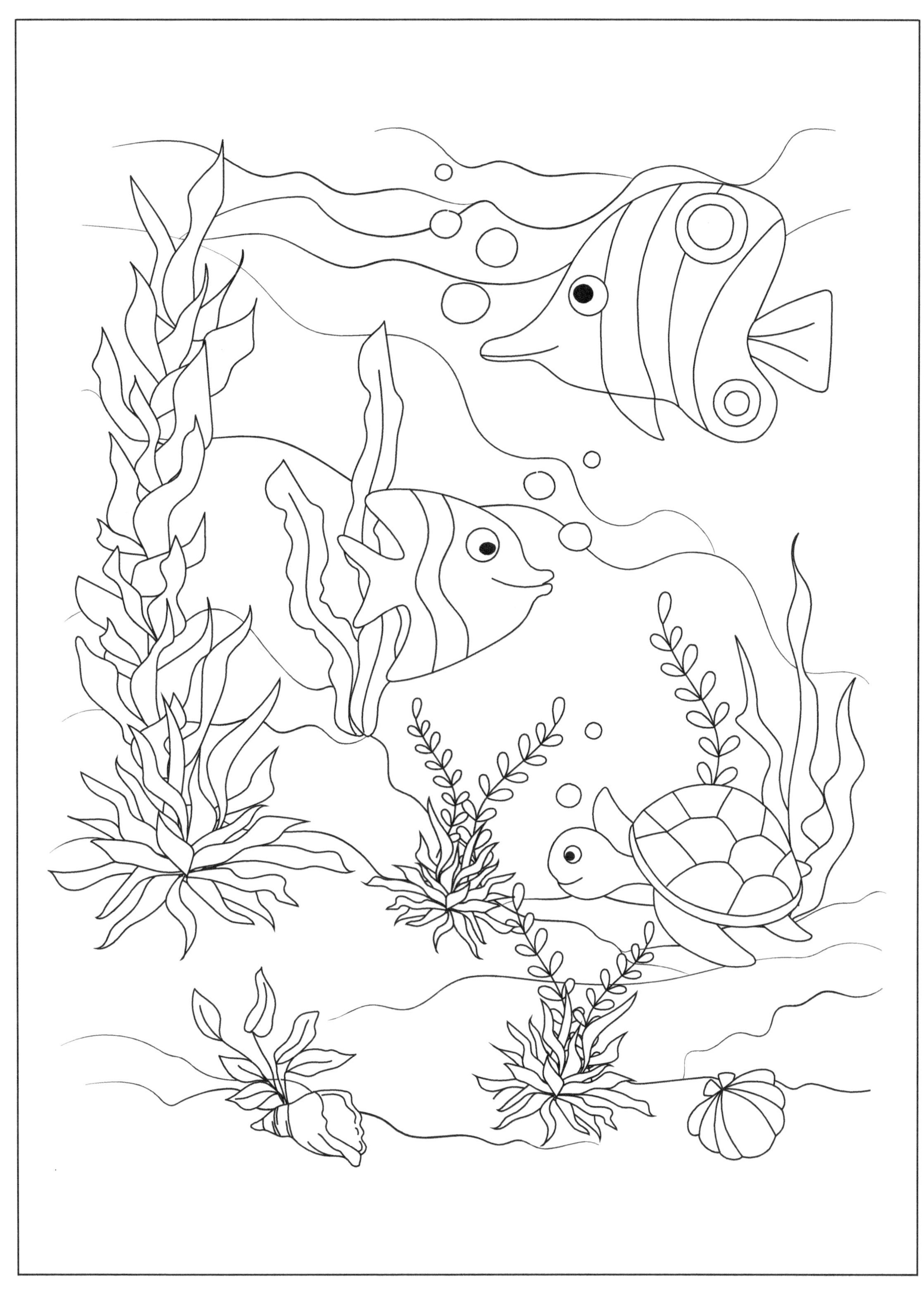

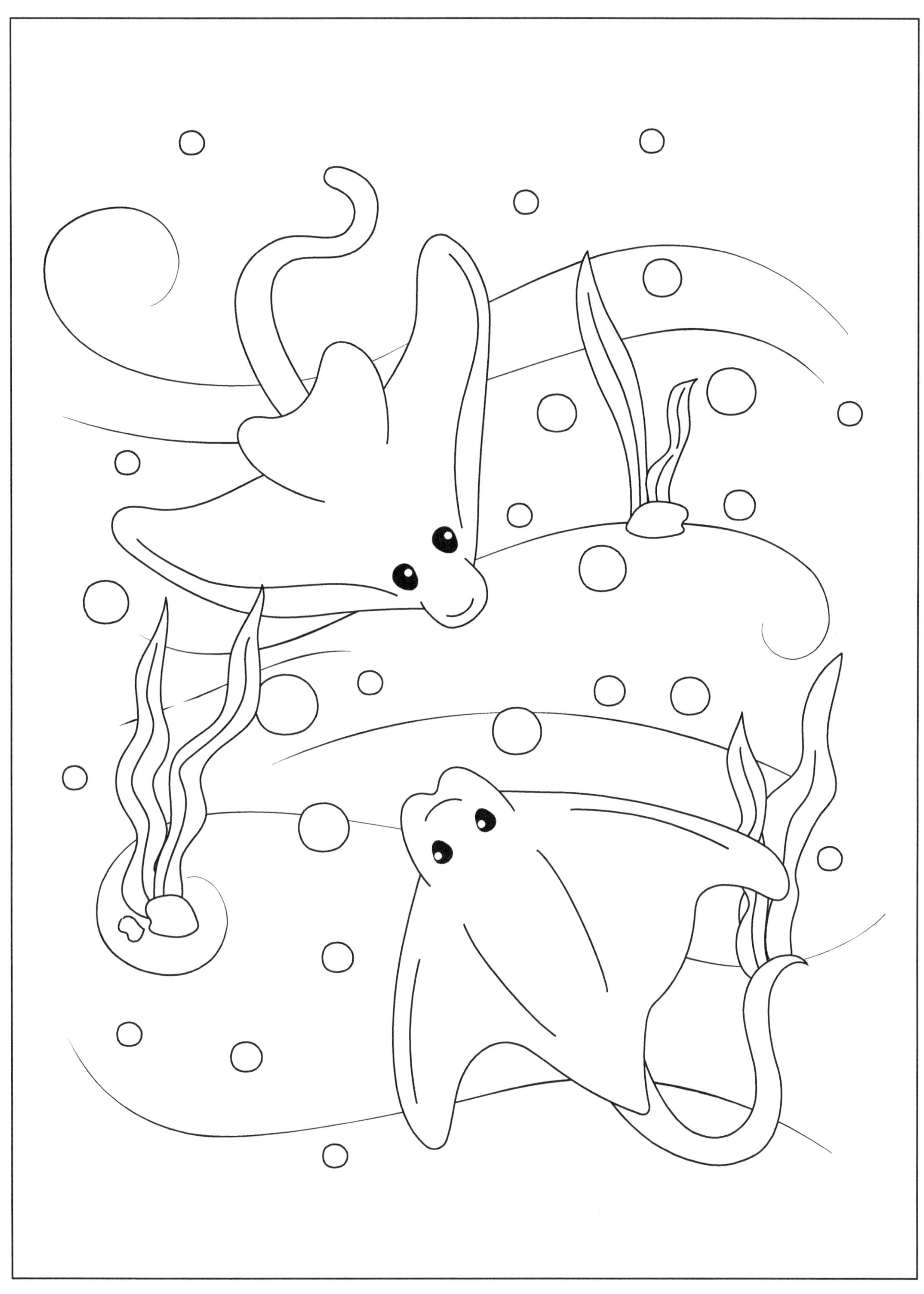

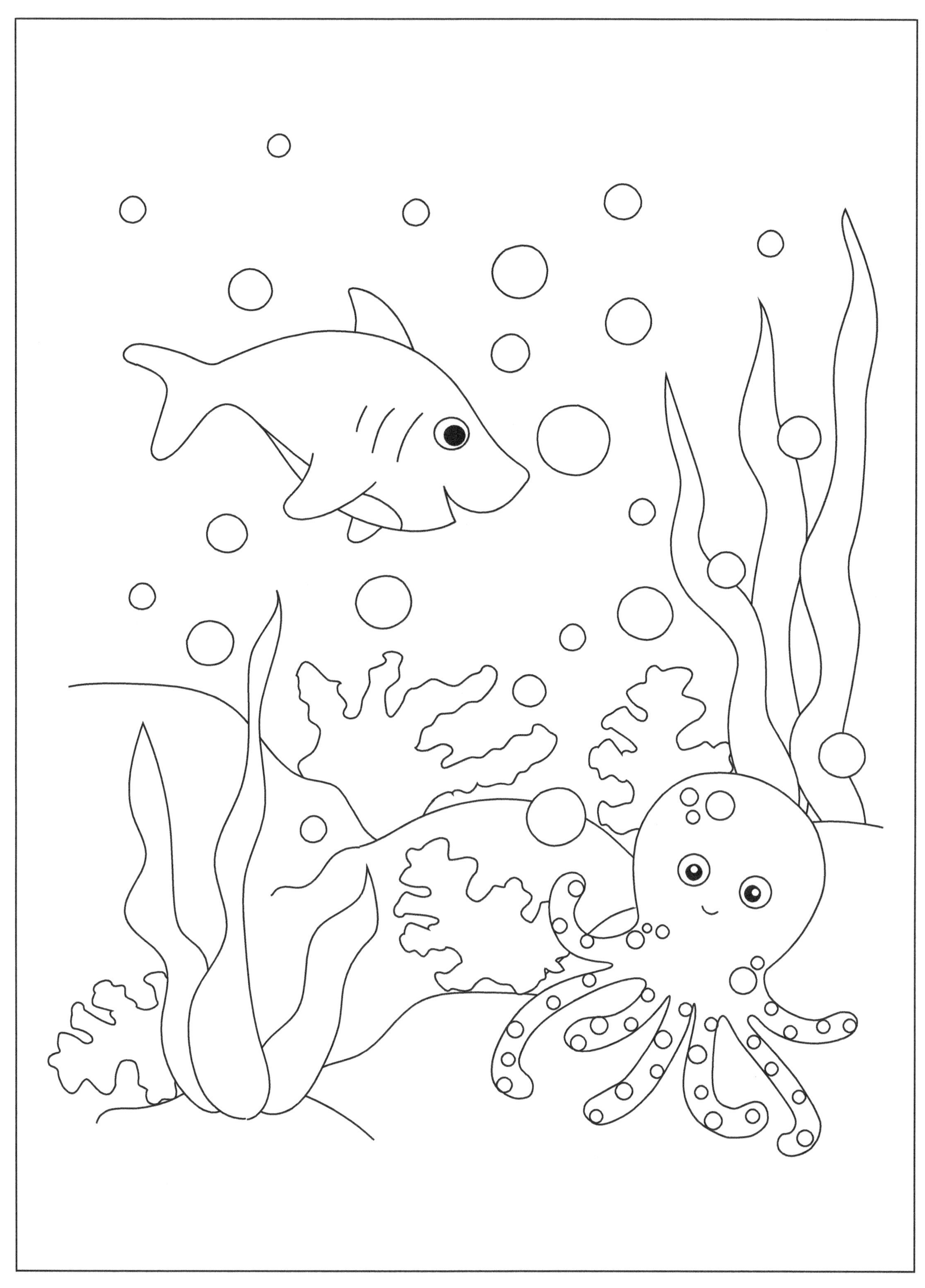

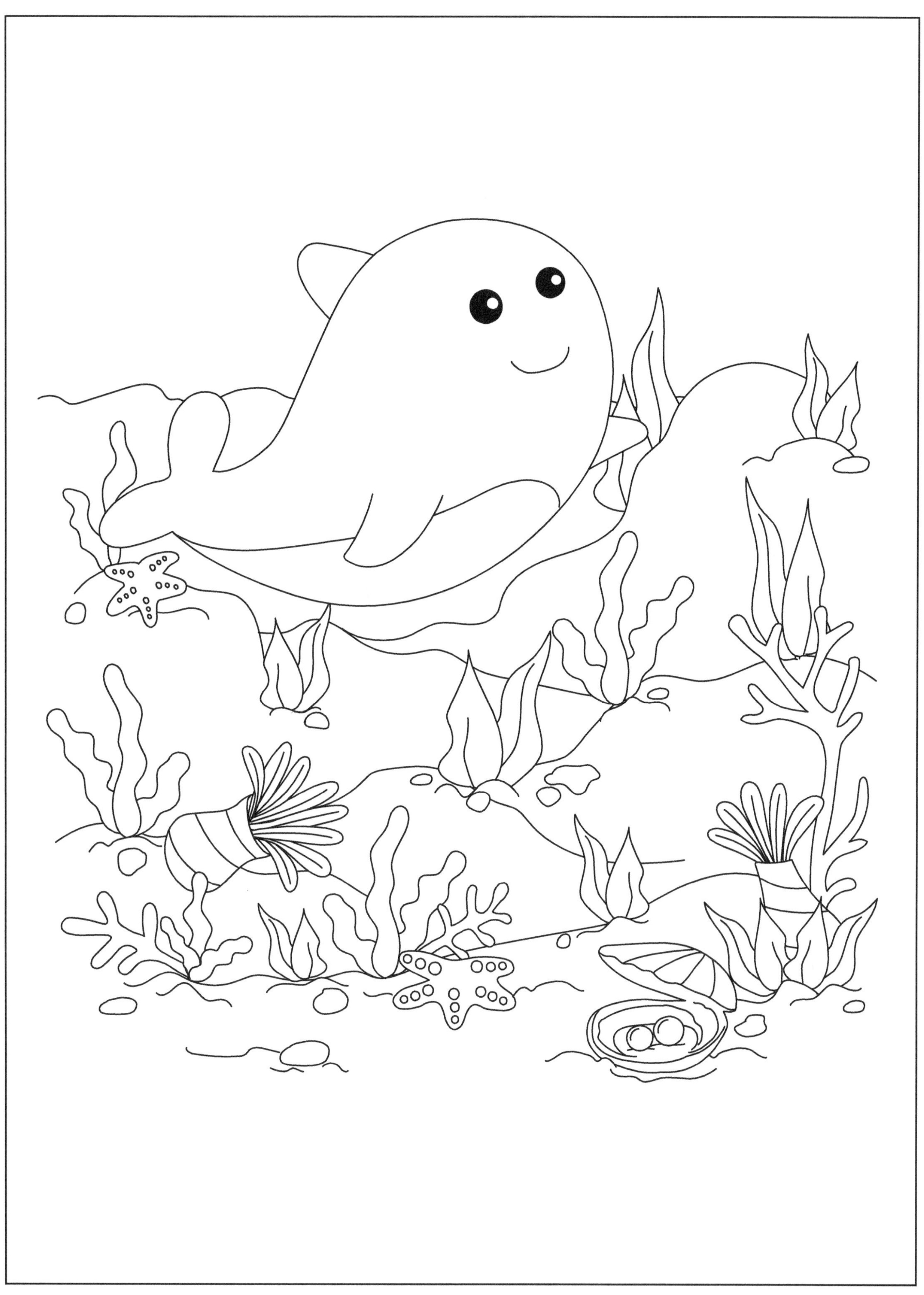

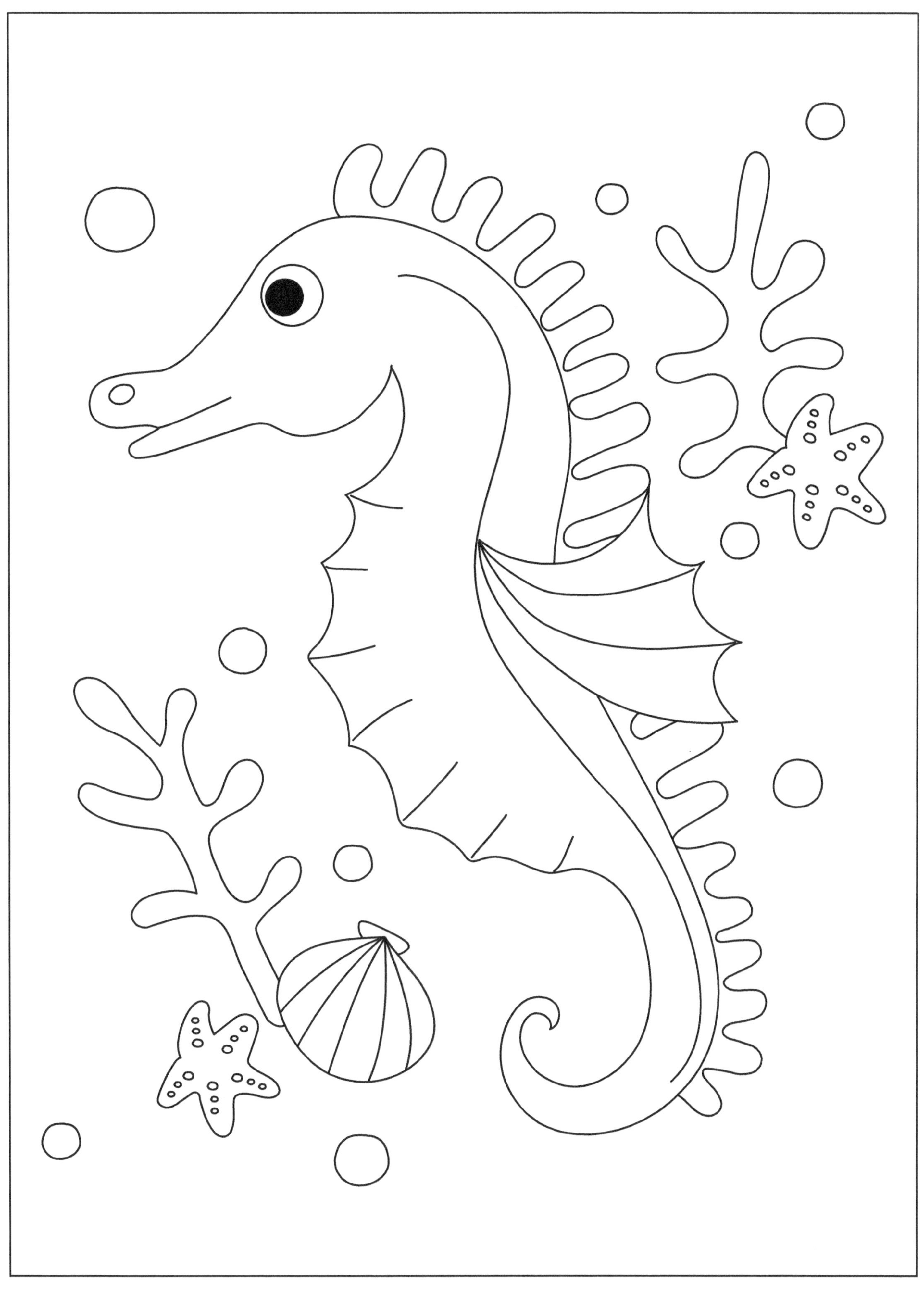

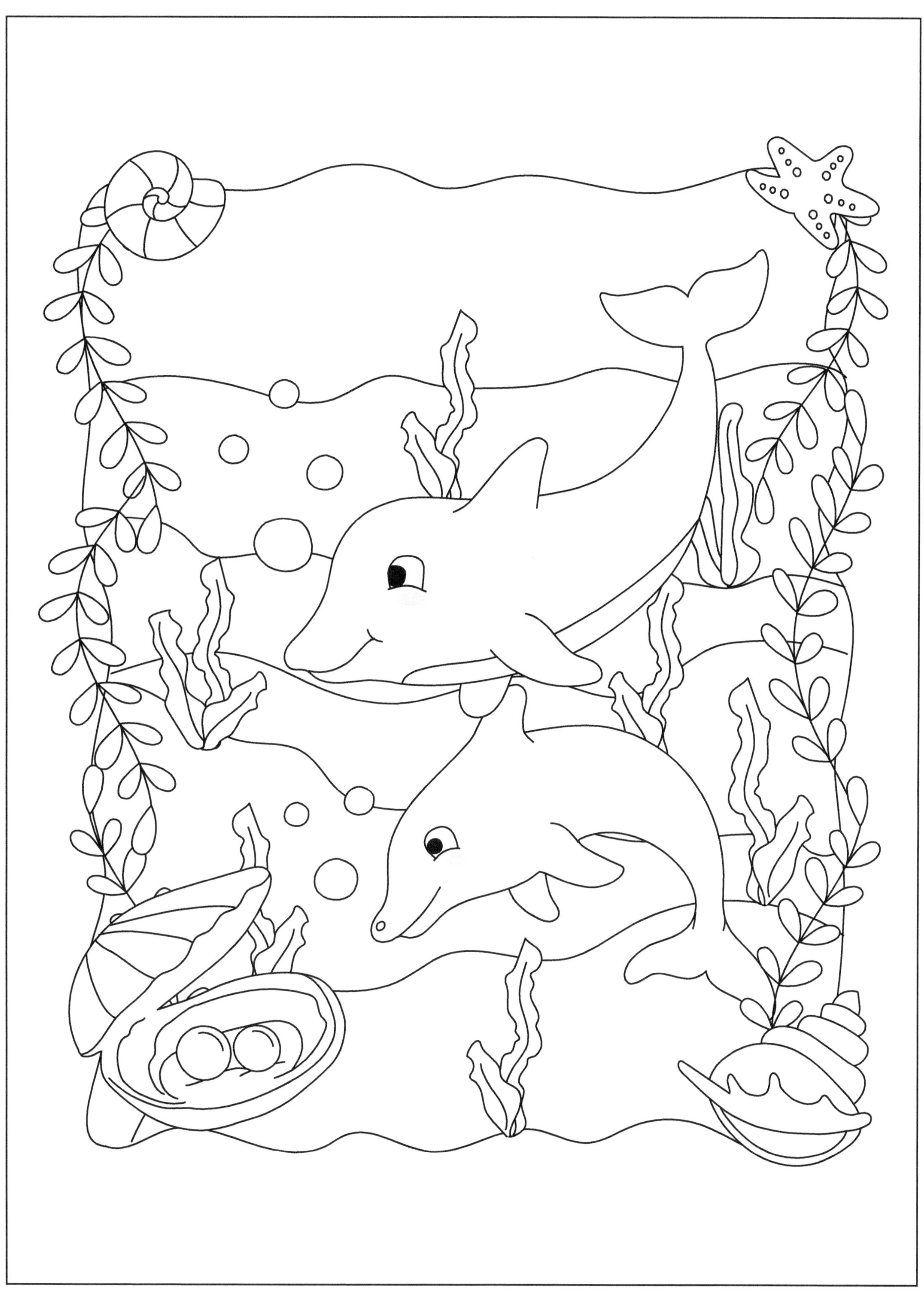

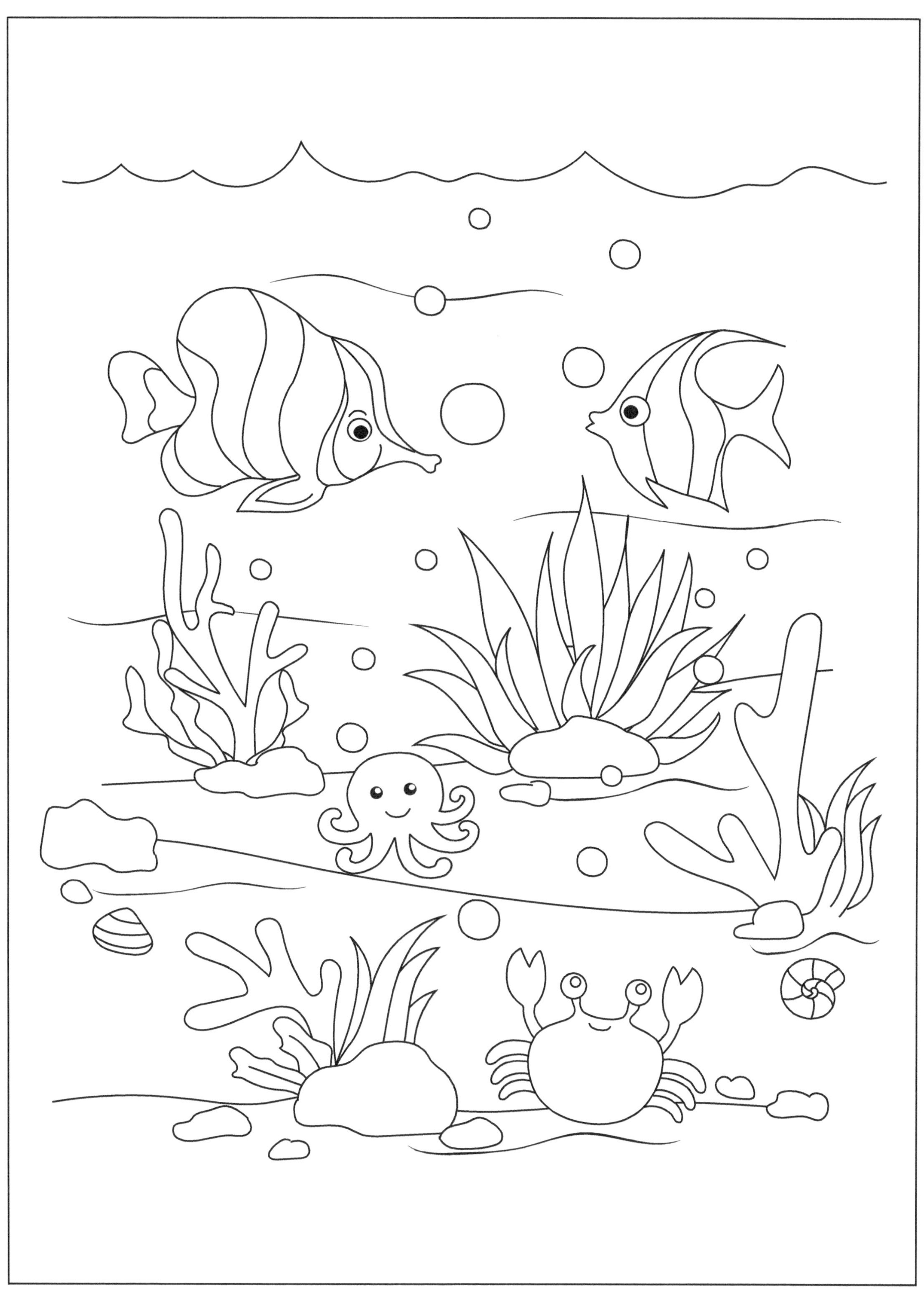

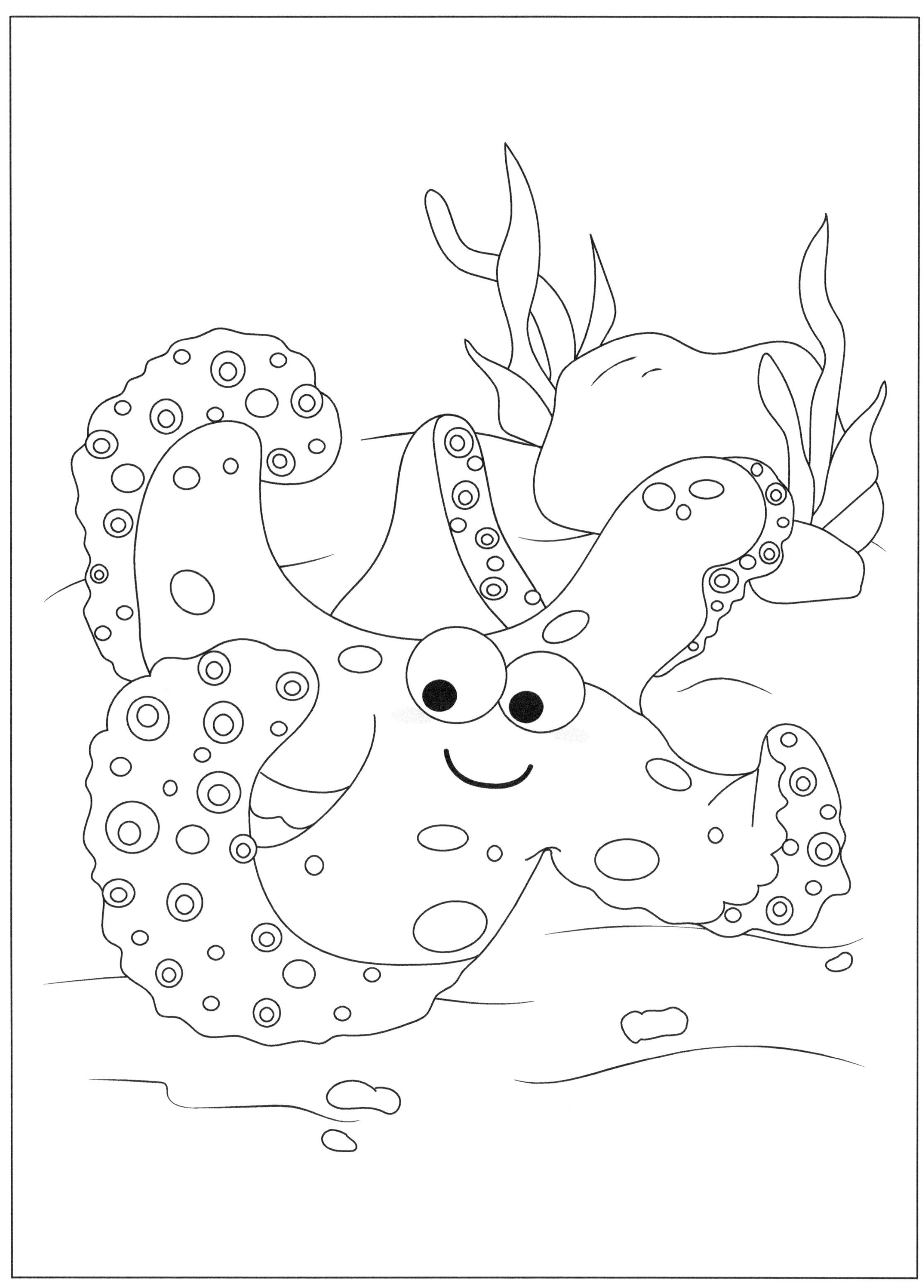

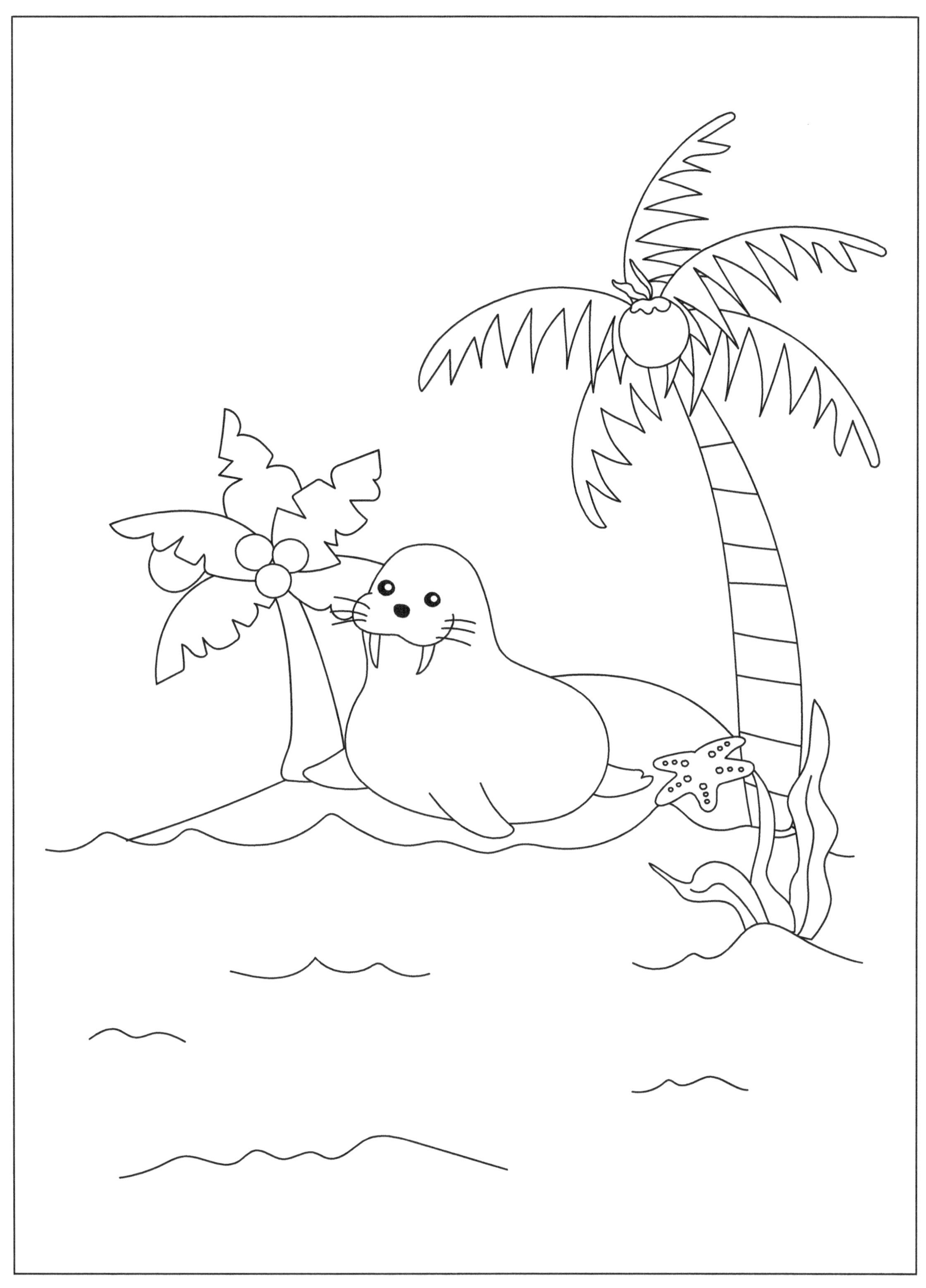

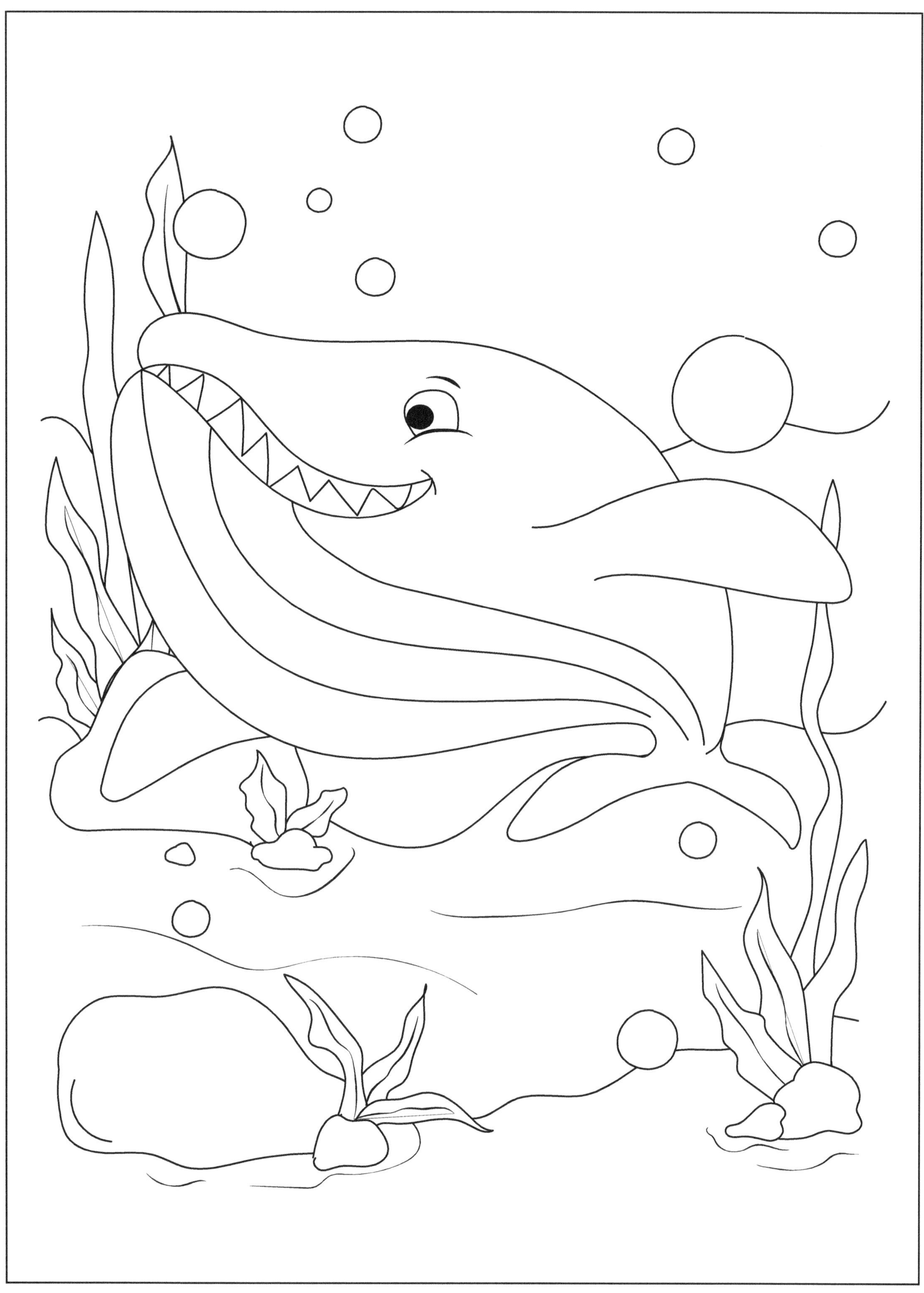

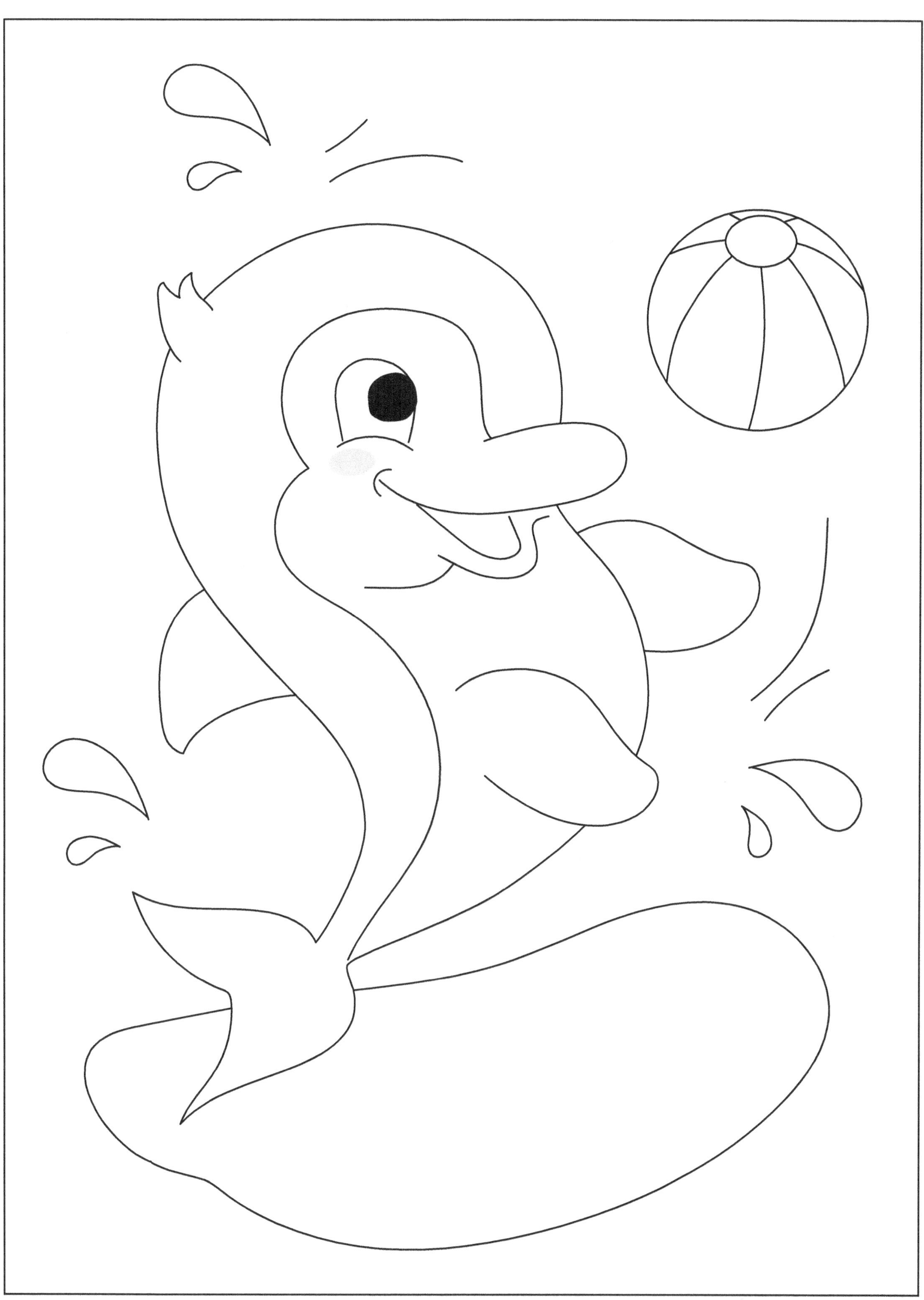

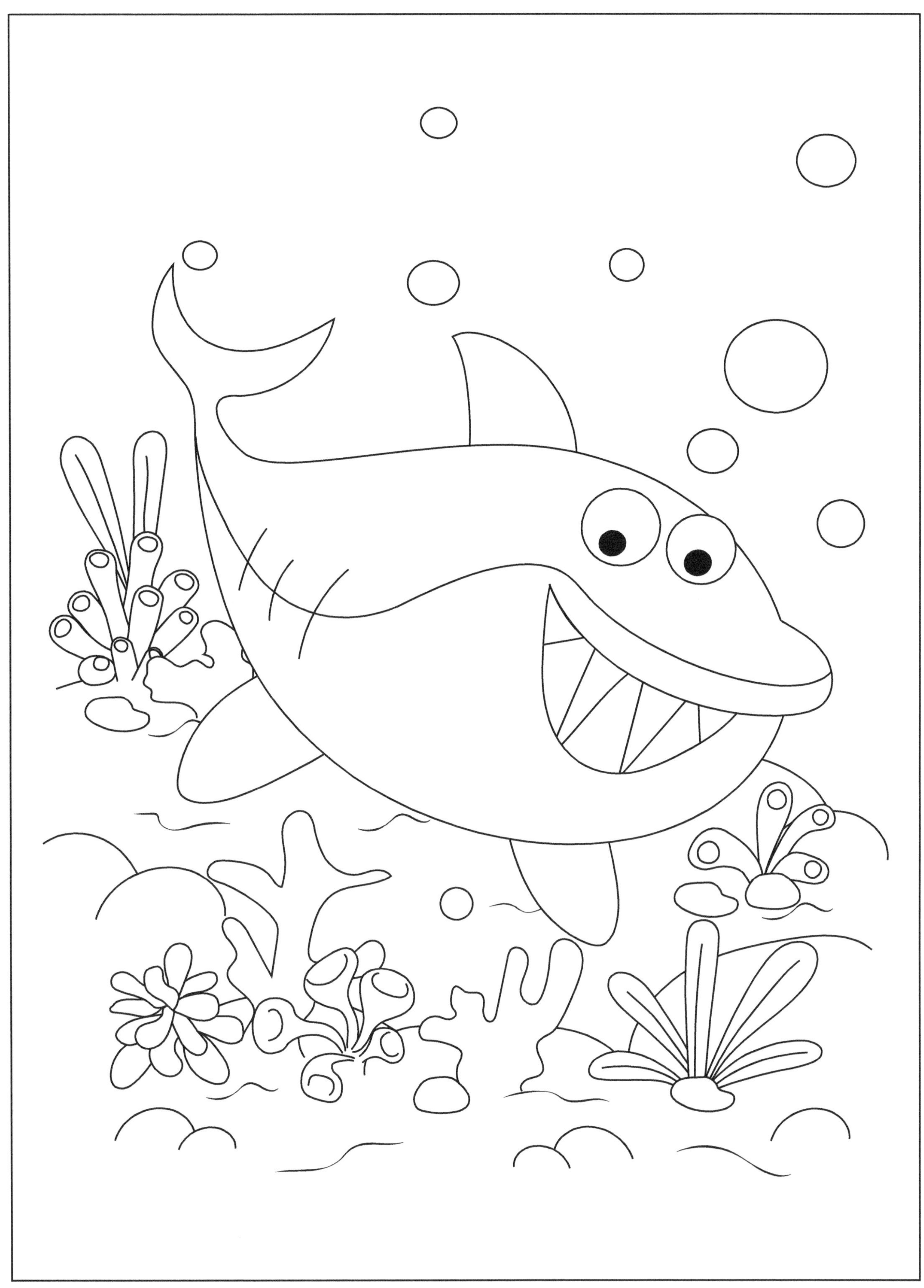

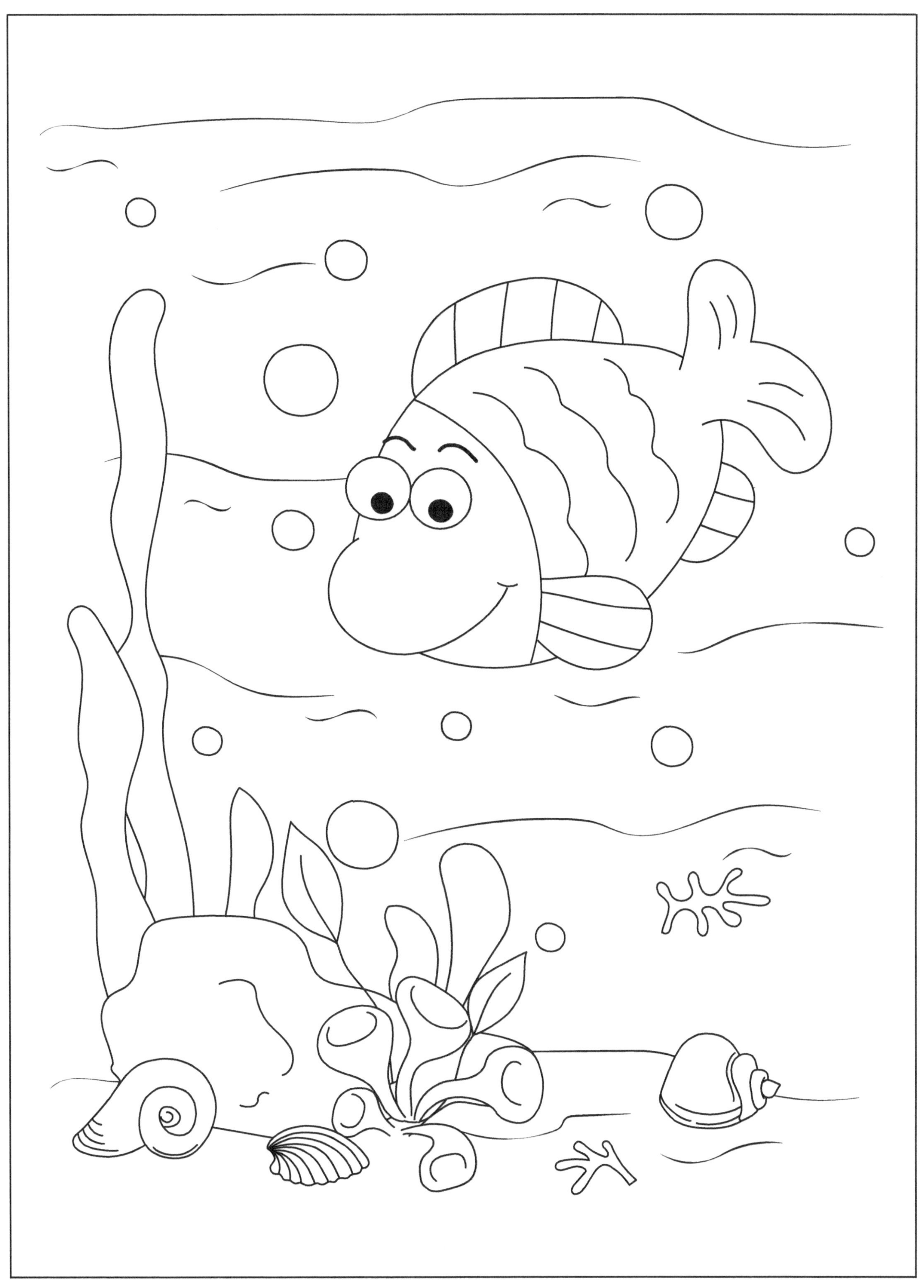

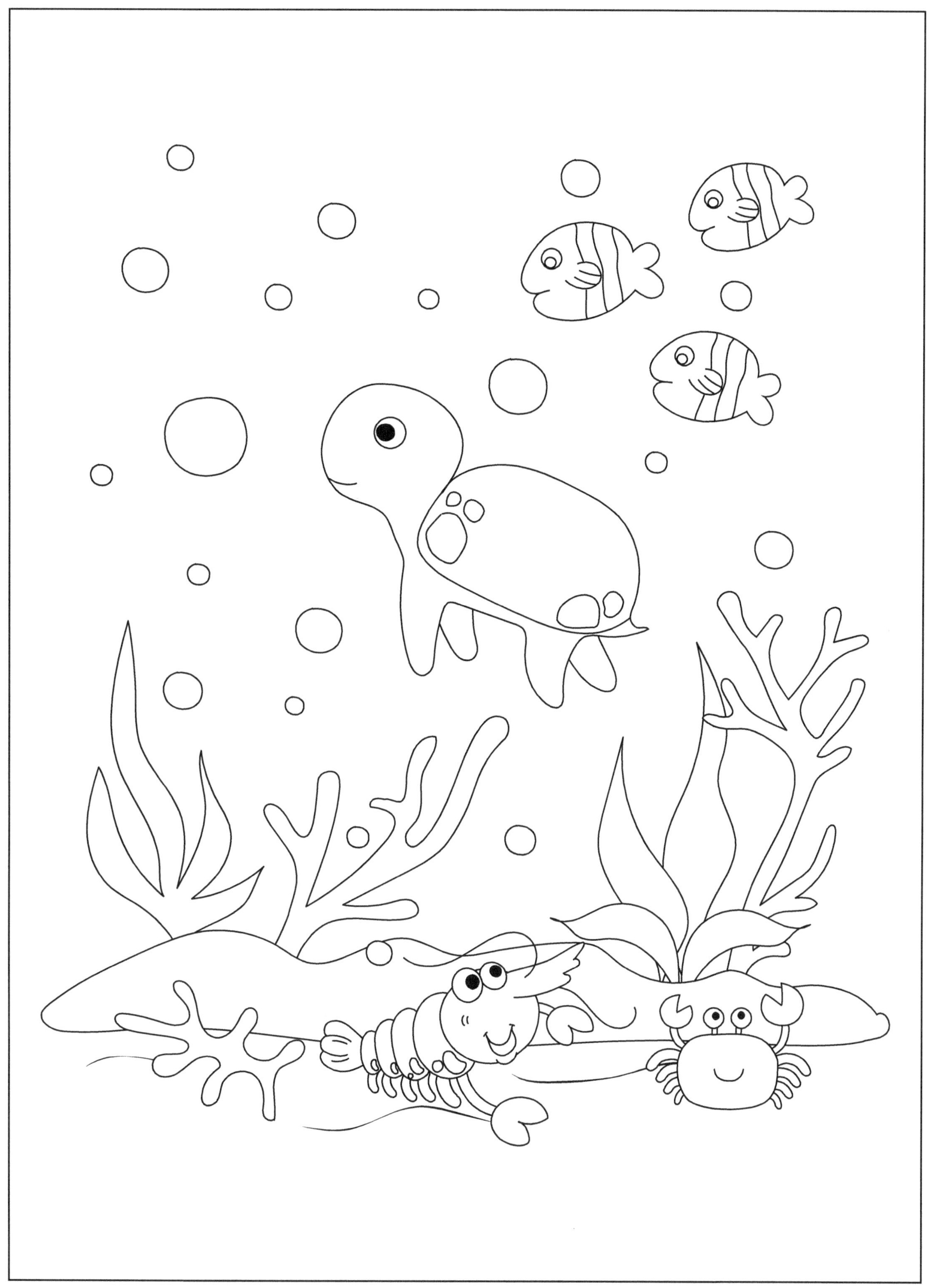

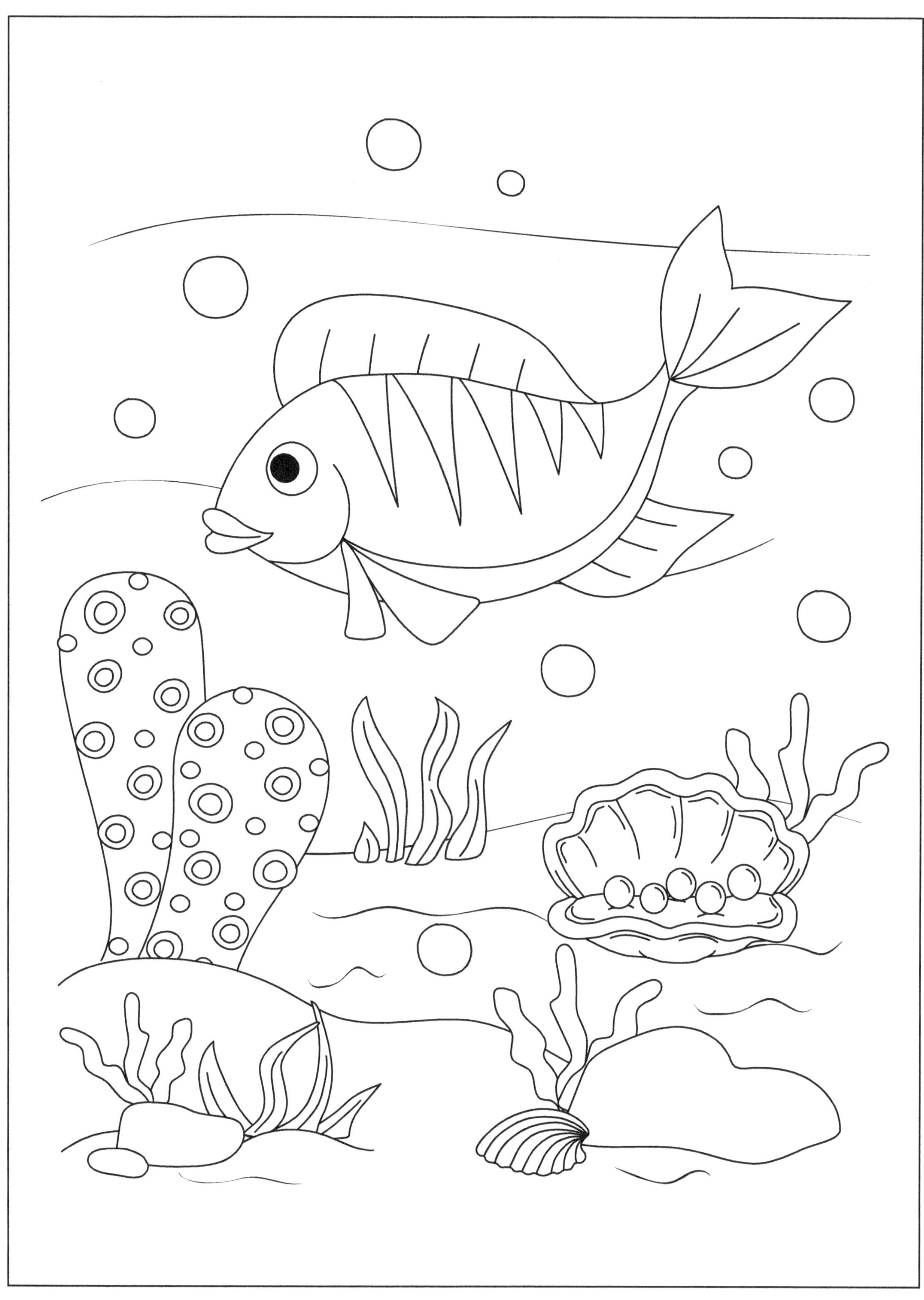

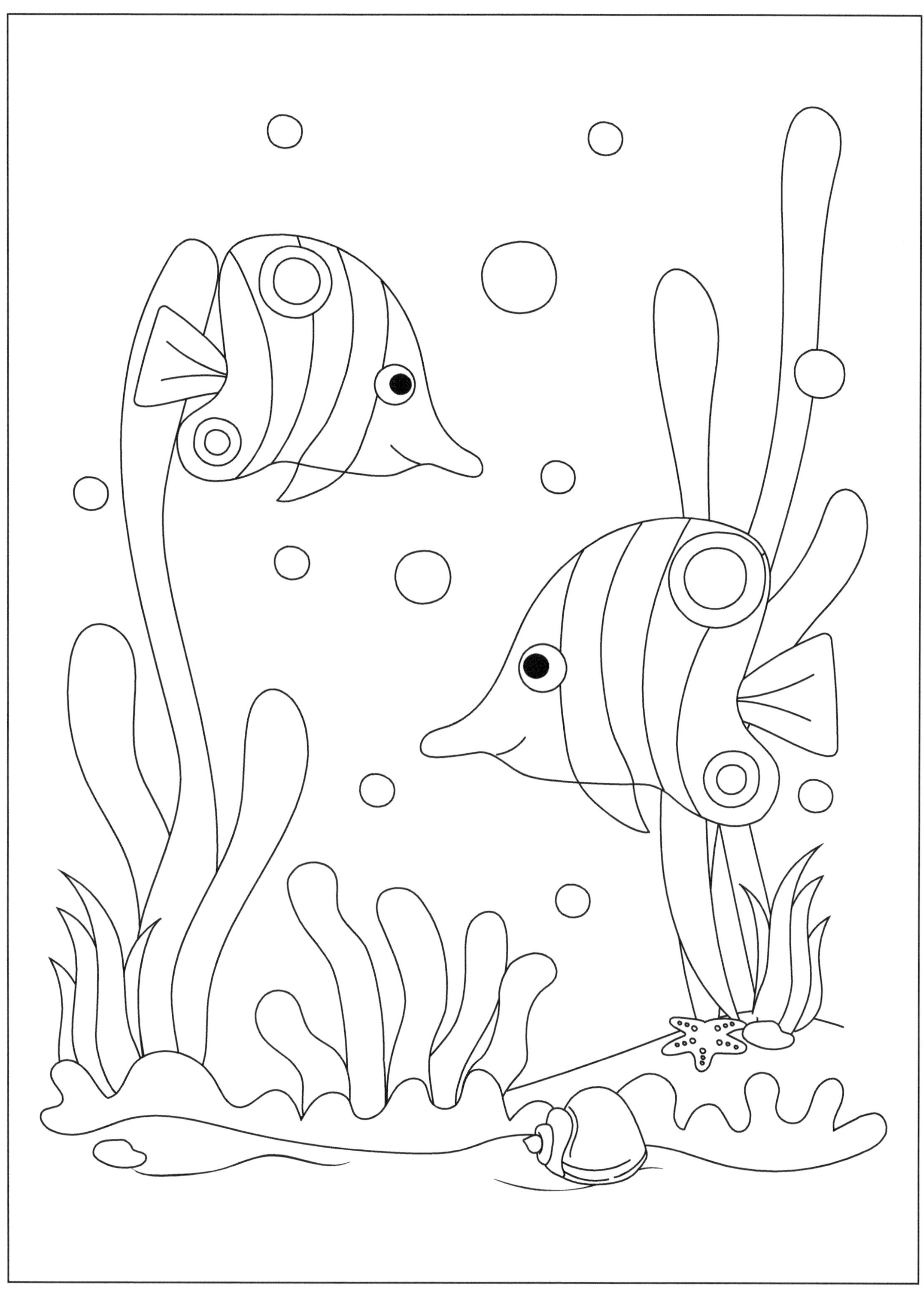

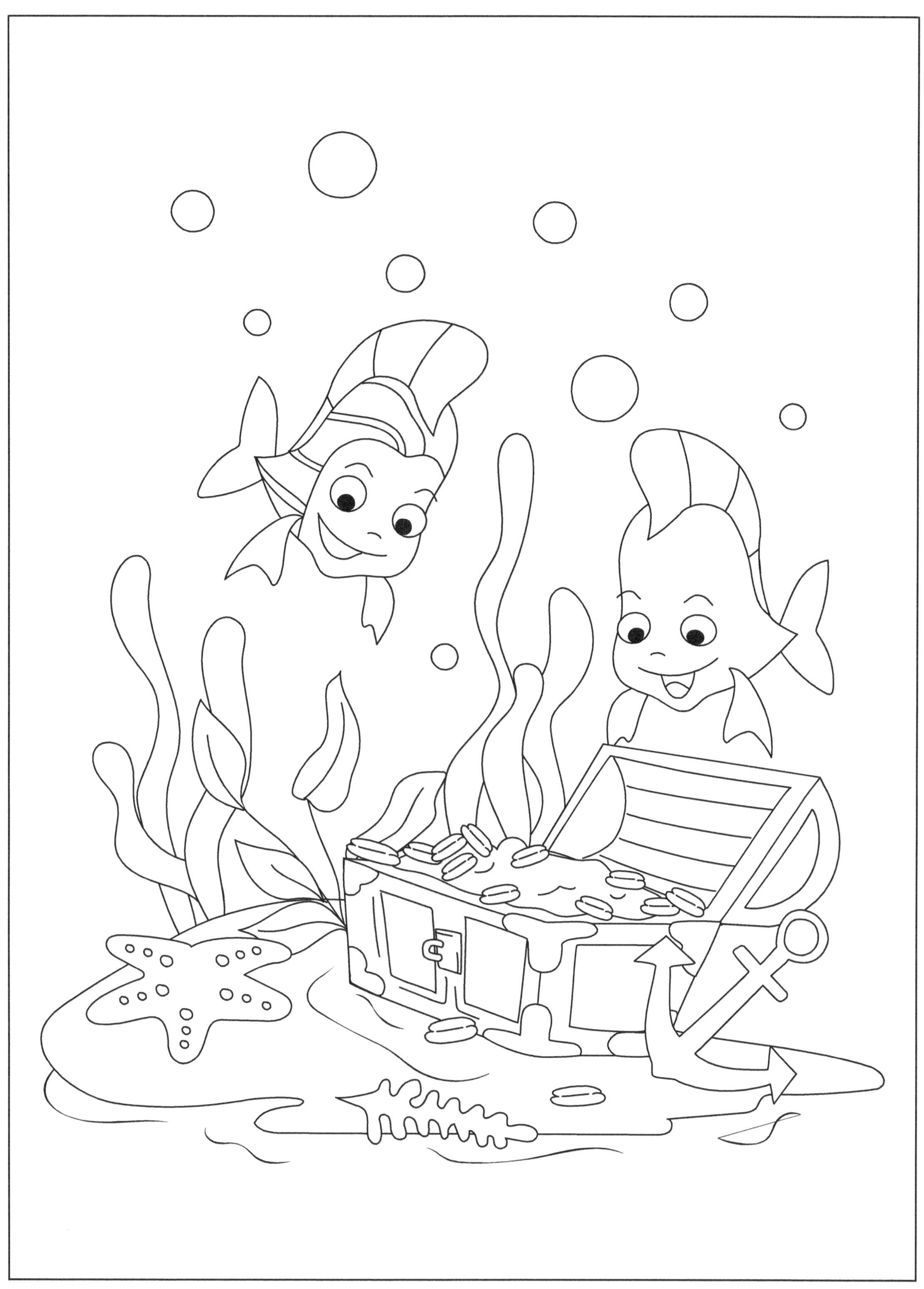

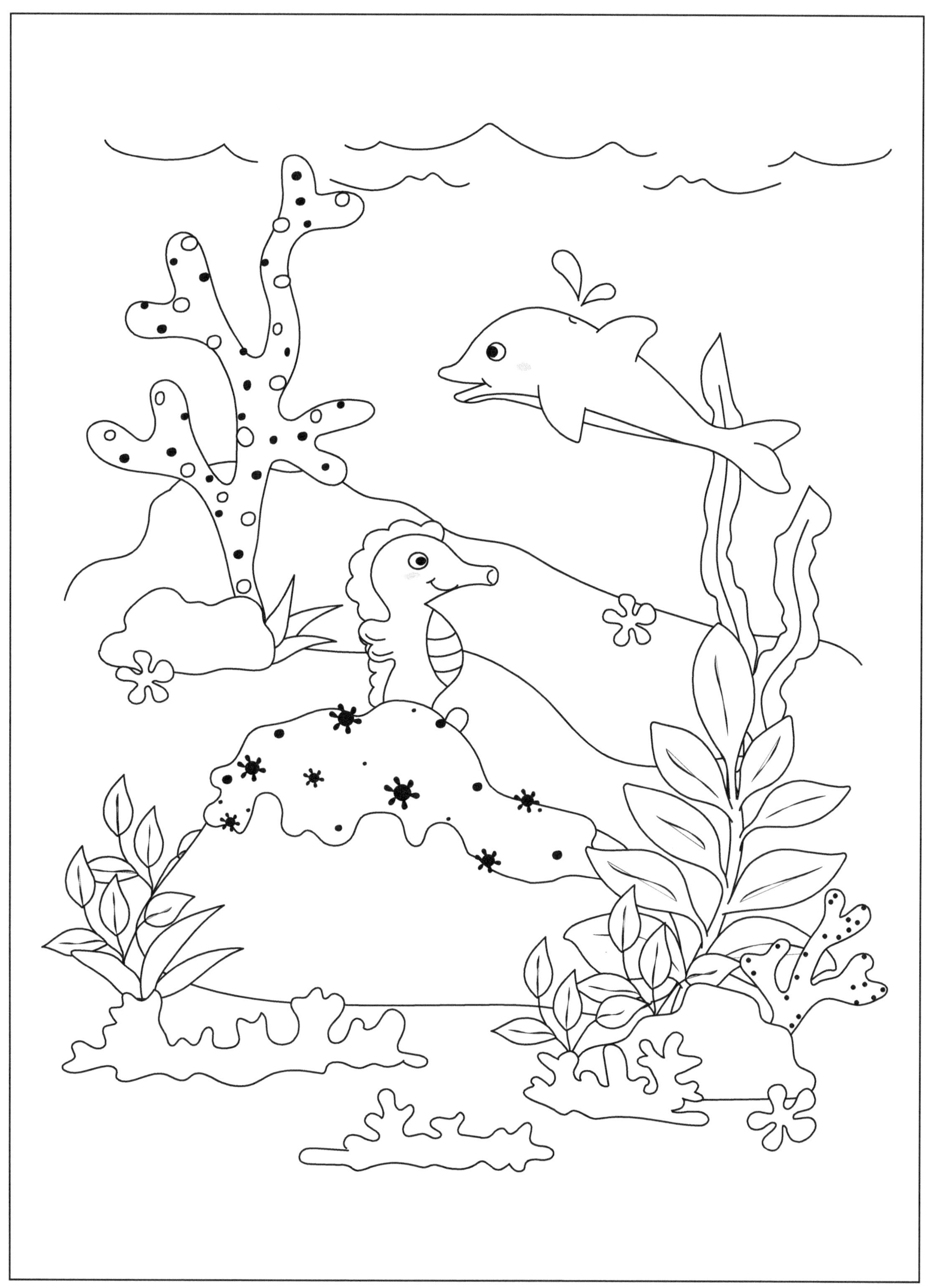

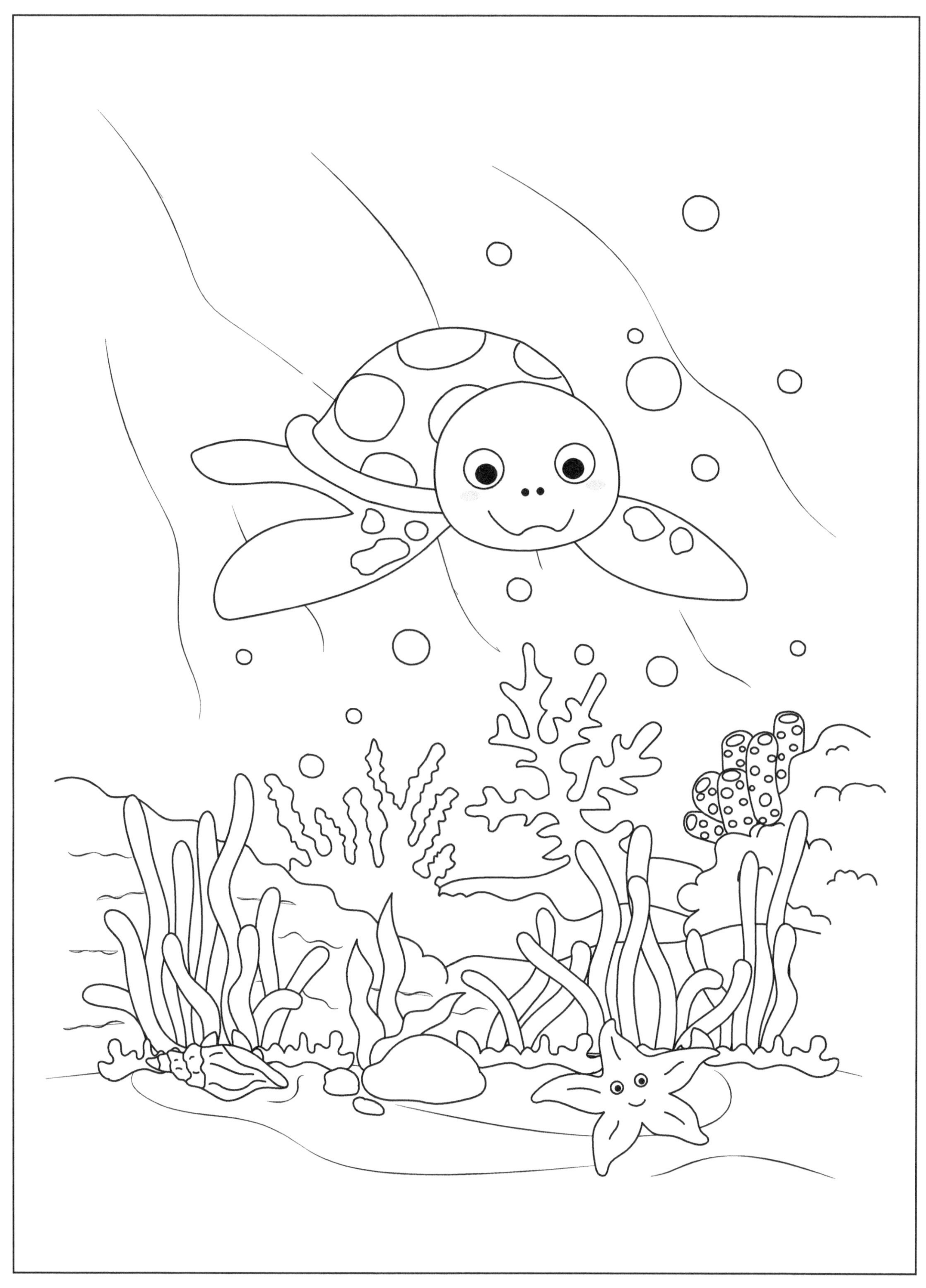

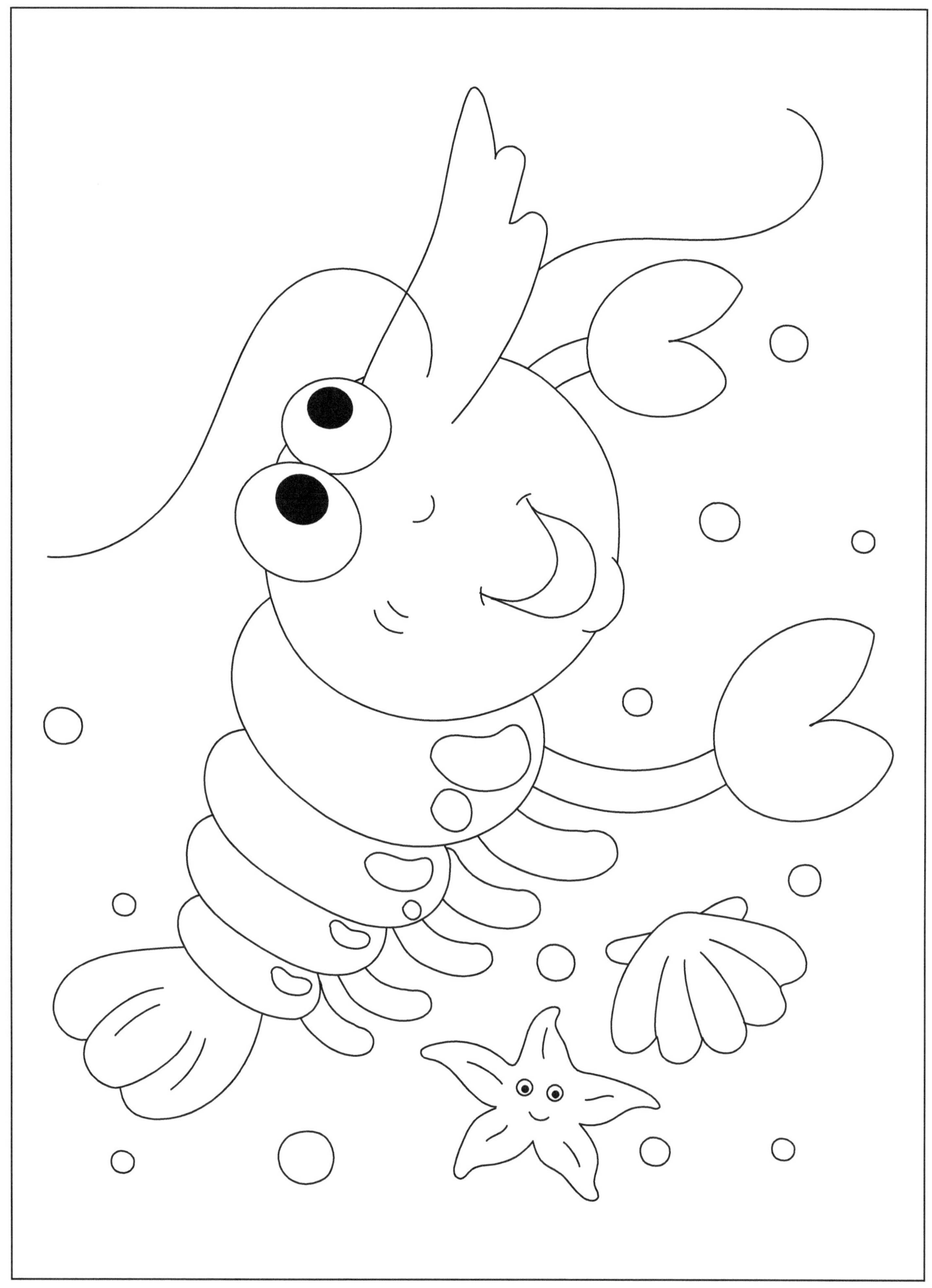

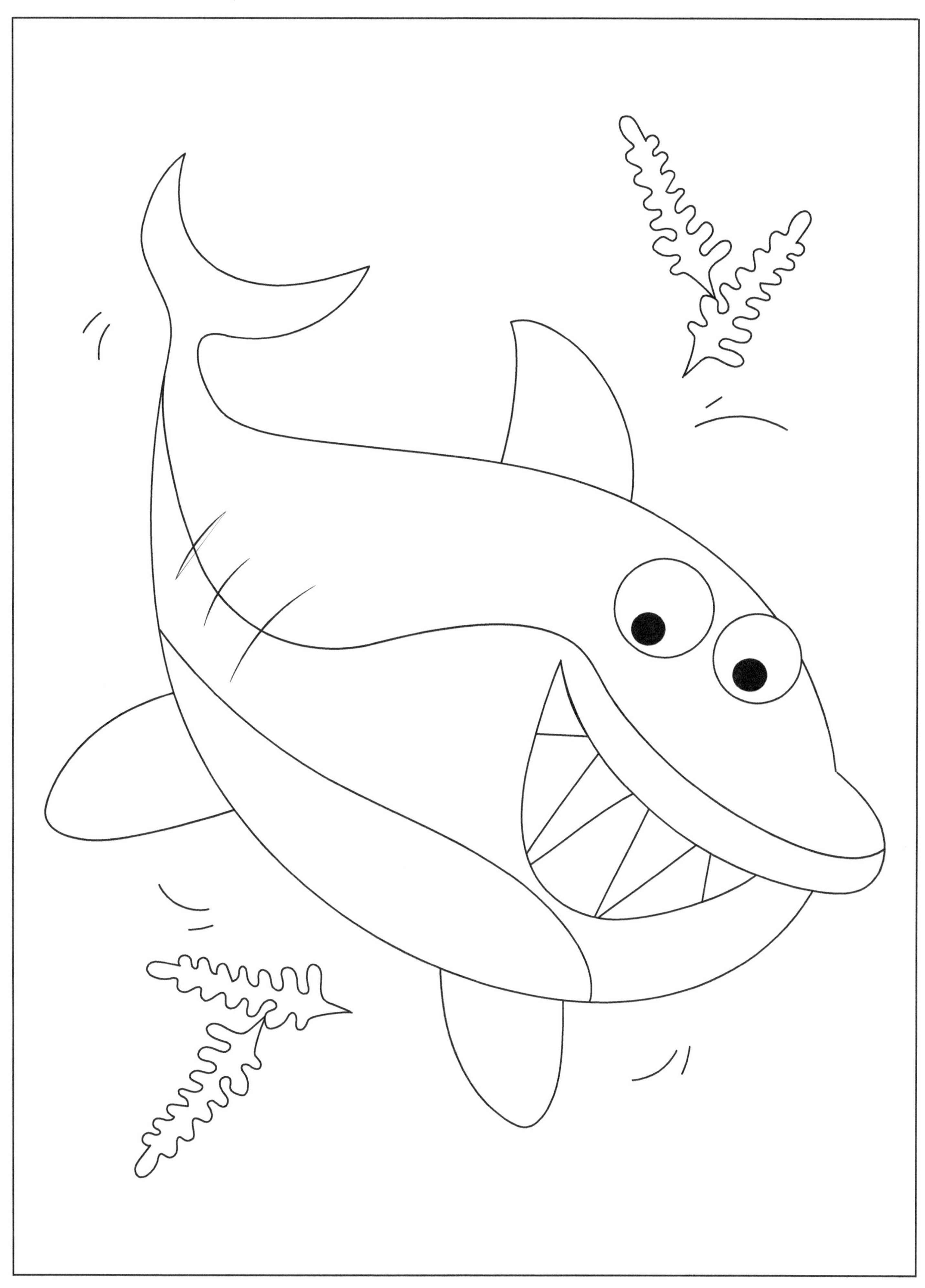

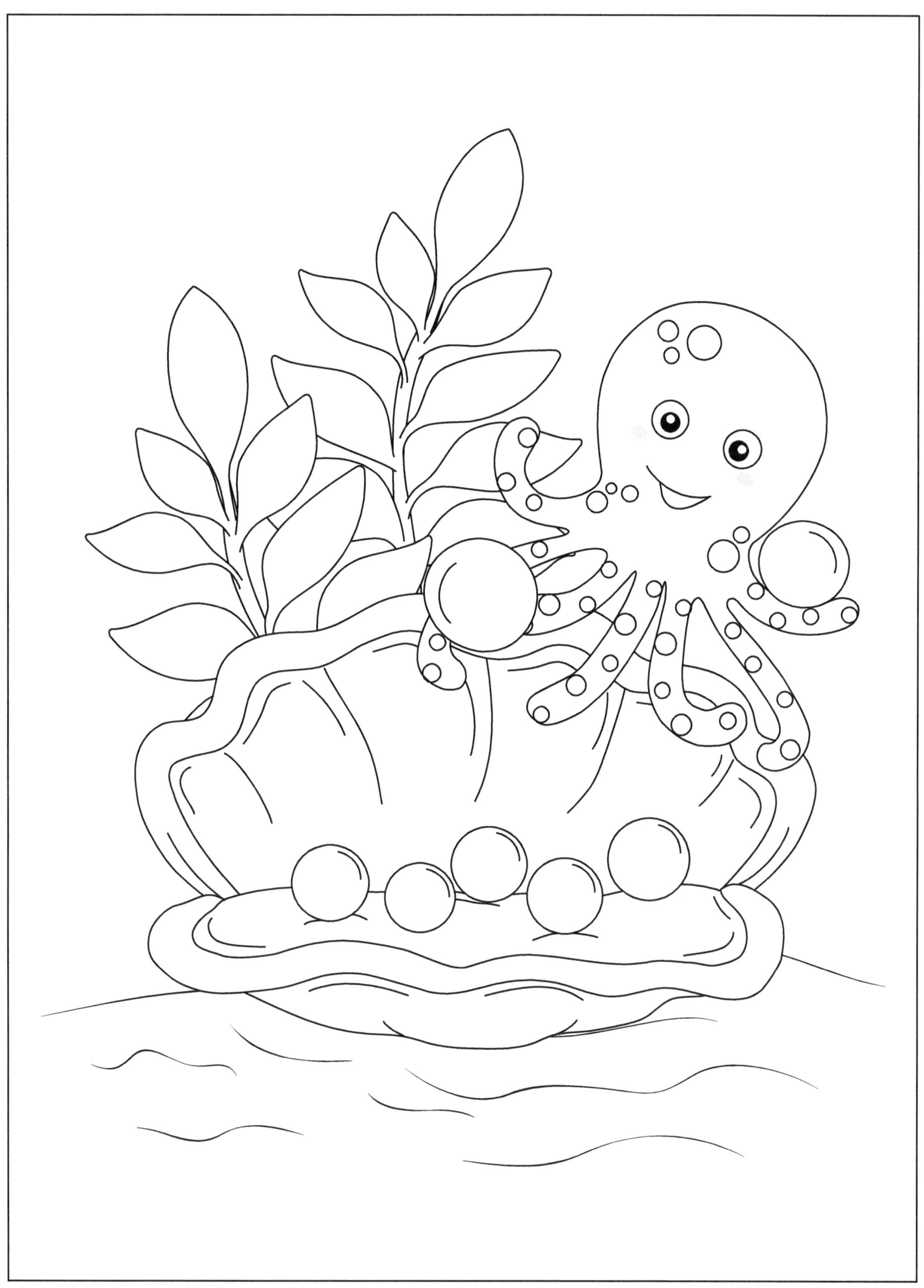

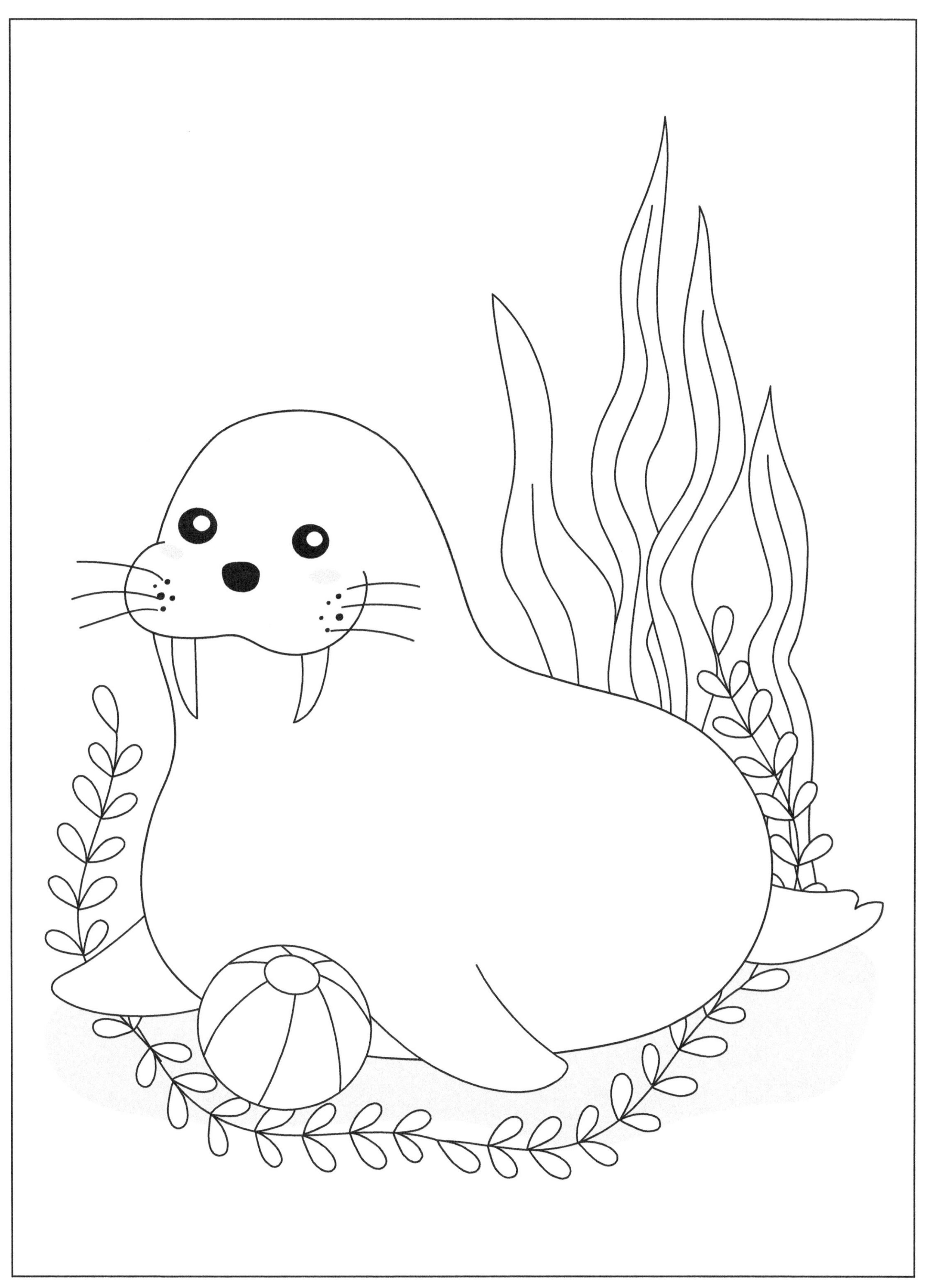

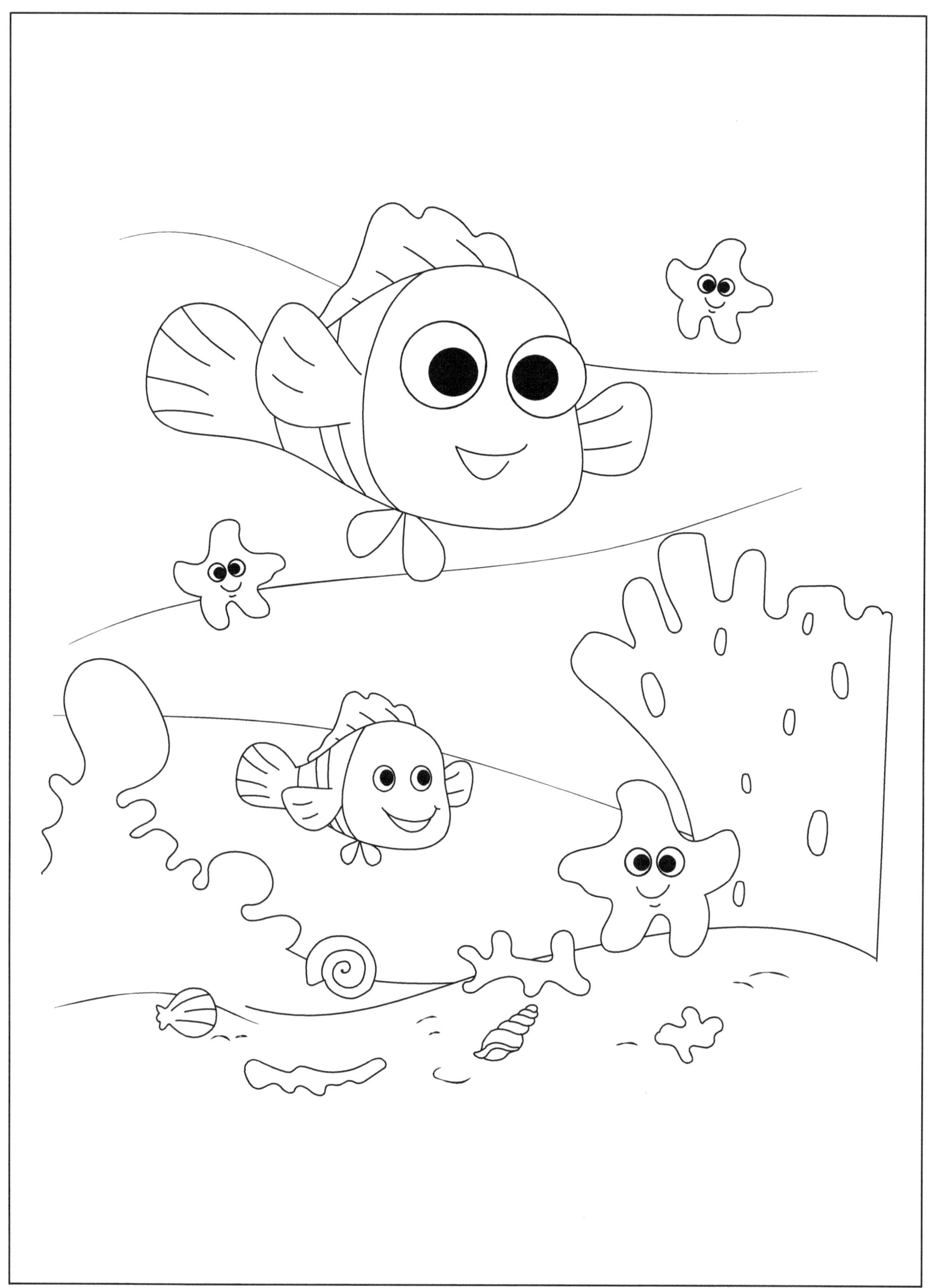

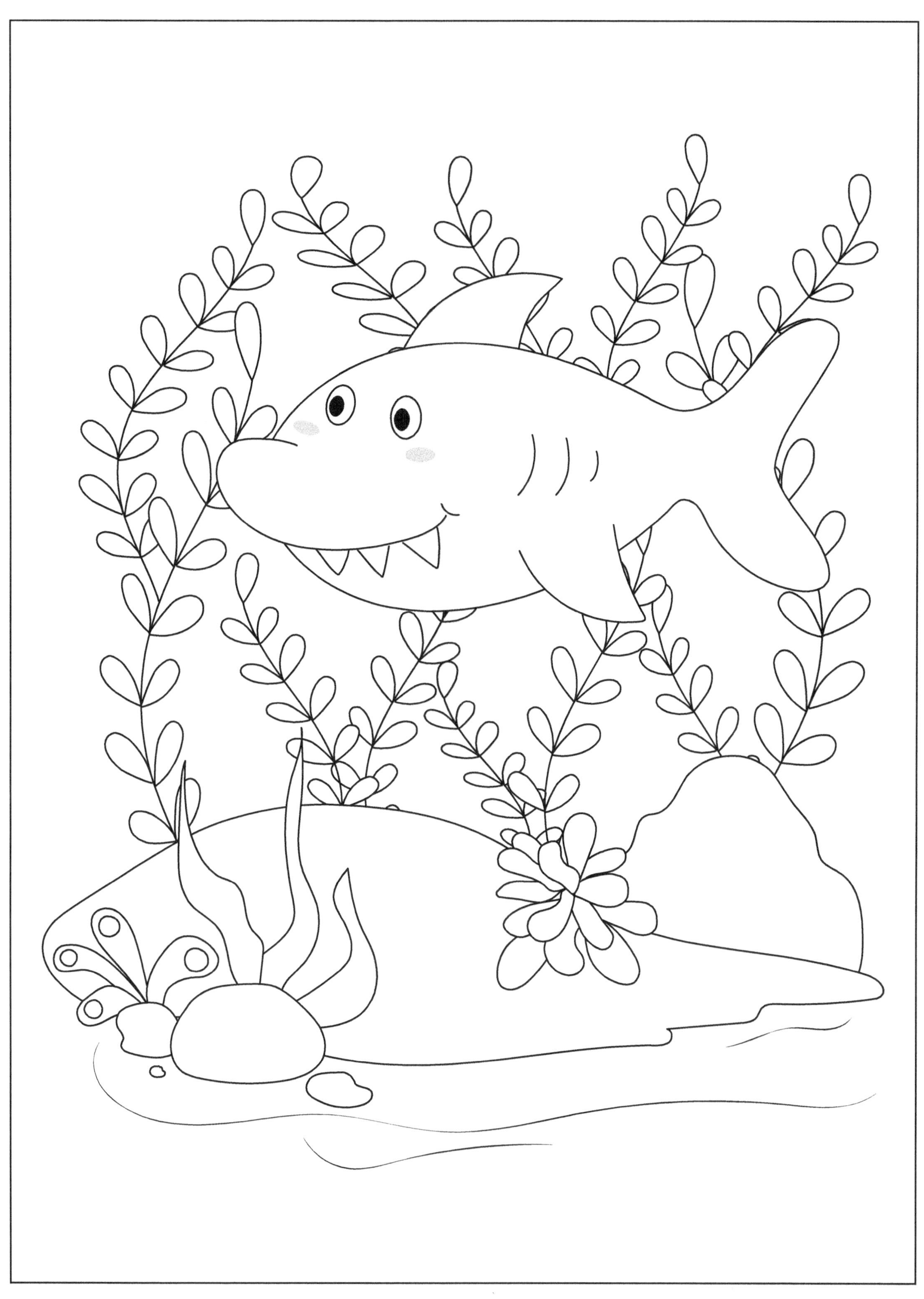

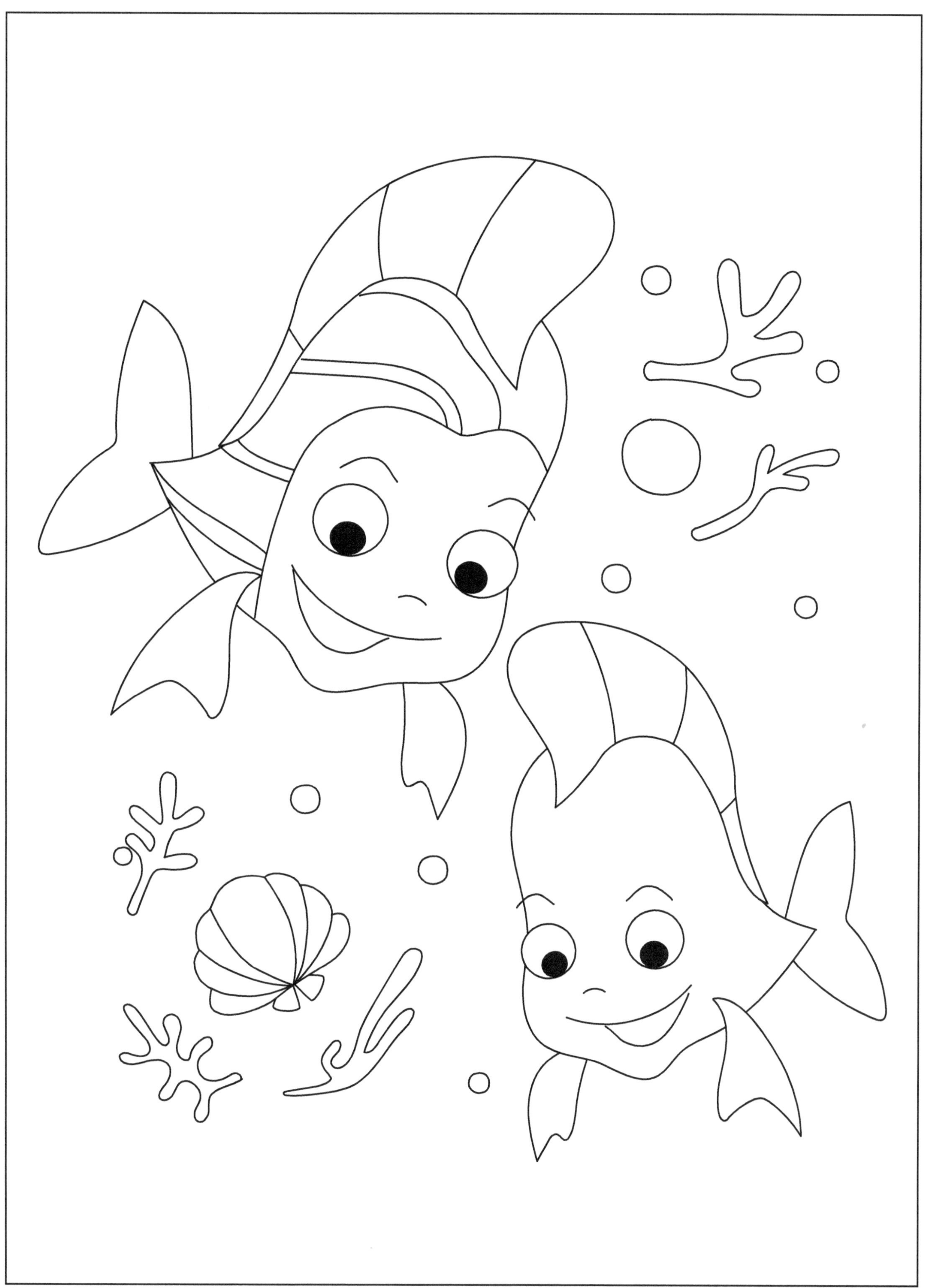